Field Hospital and Flying Column

Being the
Journal of an English Nursing Sister
in Belgium & Russia

By
Violetta Thurstan

London and New York
G. P. Putnam's Sons
1915

First Impression April 1915

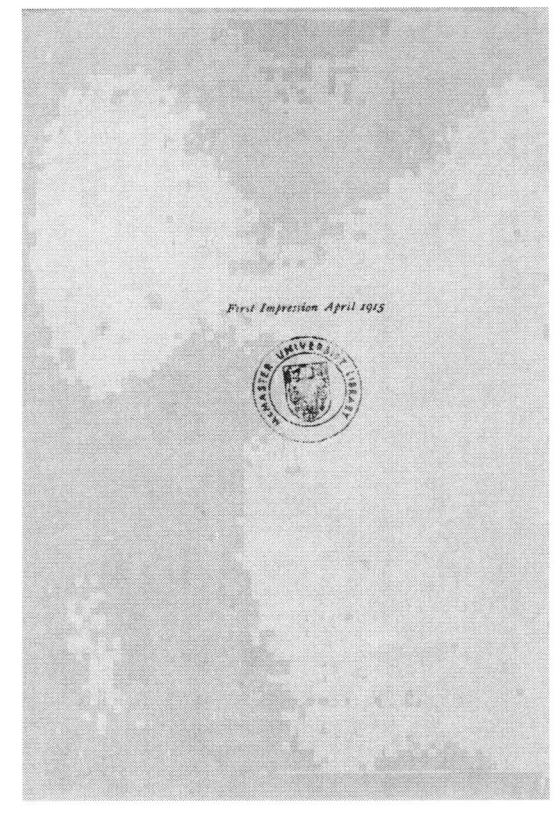

Printing Statement:

Due to the very old age and scarcity of this book, many of the pages may be hard to read due to the blurring of the original text, possible missing pages, missing text, dark backgrounds and other issues beyond our control.

Because this is such an important and rare work, we believe it is best to reproduce this book regardless of its original condition.

Thank you for your understanding.

M. R.

*Allons! After the great Companions, and to
  belong to them.*
They too are on the road.
*They are the swift and majestic men, they are
  the greatest women.*
*They know the universe itself as a road, as
  many roads,*
As roads for travelling souls.
Camerados, I will give you my hand,
I give you my love more precious than money.
*Will you give me yourselves, will you come
  travel with me?*
Shall we stick by each other as long as we live?

Contents

CHAP.		PAGE
I.	THE BEGINNING OF IT ALL	1
II.	CHARLEROI AND ROUND ABOUT	16
III.	OUR HOSPITAL AND PATIENTS	37
IV.	THE RETURN TO BRUSSELS	53
V.	A MEMORABLE JOURNEY	76
VI.	A PEACEFUL INTERLUDE	92
VII.	OUR WORK IN WARSAW	113
VIII.	THE BOMBARDMENT OF LODZ	128
IX.	MORE DOINGS OF THE FLYING COLUMN	144
X.	BY THE TRENCHES AT RADZIVILOW	161
	INDEX	179

I

THE BEGINNING OF IT ALL

WAR, war, war. For me the beginning of the war was a torchlight tattoo on Salisbury Plain. It was held on one of those breathless evenings in July when the peace of Europe was trembling in the balance, and when most of us had a heartache in case— *in case* England, at this time of internal crisis, did not rise to the supreme sacrifice.

It was just the night for a tattoo—dark and warm and still. Away across the plain a sea of mist was rolling, cutting us off from the outside world, and only a few pale stars lighted our stage from above.

The field was hung round with Chinese lanterns throwing weird lights and shadows over the mysterious forms of men and beasts that moved therein. It was fascinating to watch the stately entrance into the field, Lancers, Irish Rifles, Welsh Fusiliers,

Field Hospital & Flying Column

Grenadiers and many another gallant regiment, each marching into the field in turn to the swing of their own particular regimental tune until they were all drawn up in order.

There followed a very fine exhibition of riding and the usual torchlight tricks, and then the supreme moment came. The massed bands had thundered out the first verse of the Evening Hymn, the refrain was taken up by a single silver trumpet far away—a sweet thin almost unearthly note more to be felt than heard—and then the bands gathered up the whole melody and everybody sang the last verse together.

The Last Post followed, and then I think somehow we all knew.

*   *   *   *

A week later I had a telegram from the Red Cross summoning me to London.

London was a hive of ceaseless activity. Territorials were returning from their unfinished training, every South Coast train was crowded with Naval Reserve men who had been called up, every one was buying kits, getting medical comforts, and living at the Army and Navy Stores. Nurses trained

The Beginning of it All

and untrained were besieging the War Office demanding to be sent to the front, Voluntary Aid Detachment members were feverishly practising their bandaging, working parties and ambulance classes were being organized, crowds without beginning and without end were surging up and down the pavements between Westminster and Charing Cross, wearing little flags, buying every half-hour edition of the papers and watching the stream of recruits at St. Martin's. All was excitement—no one knew what was going to happen. Then the bad news began to come through from Belgium, and every one steadied down and settled themselves to their task of waiting or working, whichever it might happen to be.

I was helping at the Red Cross Centre in Vincent Square, and all day long there came an endless procession of women wanting to help, some trained nurses, many—far too many—half-trained women; and a great many raw recruits, some anxious for adventure and clamouring " to go to the front at once," others willing and anxious to do the humblest service that would be of use in this time of crisis.

Field Hospital & Flying Column

Surely after this lesson the Bill for the State Registration of Trained Nurses cannot be ignored or held up much longer. Even now in this twentieth century, girls of twenty-one, nurses so-called with six months' hospital training, somehow manage to get out to the front, blithely undertaking to do work that taxes to its very utmost the skill, endurance, and resource of the most highly trained women who have given up the best years of their life to learning the principles that underlie this most exacting of professions. For it is not only medical and surgical nursing that is learnt in a hospital ward, it is discipline, endurance, making the best of adverse circumstances, and above all the knowledge of mankind. These are the qualities that are needed at the front, and they cannot be imparted in a few bandaging classes or instructions in First Aid.

This is not a diatribe against members of Voluntary Aid Detachments. They do not, as a rule, pretend to be what they are not, and I have found them splendid workers in their own department. They are not half-trained nurses but fully trained ambulance

The Beginning of it All

workers, ready to do probationer's work under the fully trained sisters, or if necessary to be wardmaid, laundress, charwoman, or cook, as the case may be. The difficulty does not lie with them, but with the women who have a few weeks' or months' training, who blossom out into full uniform and call themselves Sister Rose, or Sister Mabel, and are taken at their own valuation by a large section of the public, and manage through influence or bluff to get posts that should only be held by trained nurses, and generally end by bringing shame and disrepute upon the profession.

* * * * *

The work in the office was diversified by a trip to Faversham with some very keen and capable Voluntary Aid Detachment members, to help improvise a temporary hospital for some Territorials who had gone sick. And then my turn came for more active service. I was invited by the St. John Ambulance to take out a party of nurses to Belgium for service under the Belgian Red Cross Society.

Very little notice was possible, everything was arranged on Saturday afternoon of all impossible afternoons to arrange anything in London, and we were to start for Brussels at eight o'clock on Tuesday morning.

On Monday afternoon I was interviewing my nurses, saying good-bye to friends—shopping in between—wildly trying to get everything I wanted at the eleventh hour, when suddenly a message came to say that the start would not be to-morrow after all. Great excitement—telephones—wires—interviews. It seemed that there was some hitch in the arrangements at Brussels, but at last it was decided by the St. John's Committee that I should go over alone the next day to see the Belgian Red Cross authorities before the rest of the party were sent off. The nurses were to follow the day after if it could be arranged, as having been all collected in London, it was very inconvenient for them to be kept waiting long.

Early Tuesday morning saw me at Charing Cross Station. There were not many people crossing—two well-known surgeons on their way to Belgium, Major Richardson with his war-dogs, and a few others. A nurse going to Antwerp, with myself, formed the only female contingent on board. It was asserted

The Beginning of it All

that a submarine preceded us all the way to Ostend, but as I never get further than my berth on these occasions, I cannot vouch for the truth of this.

Ostend in the middle of August generally means a gay crowd of bathers, Cook's tourists tripping to Switzerland and so on; but our little party landed in silence, and anxious faces and ominous whispers met us on our arrival on Belgian soil. It was even said that the Germans were marching on Brussels, but this was contradicted afterwards as a sensational canard. The Red Cross on my luggage got me through the *douane* formalities without any trouble. I entered the almost empty train and we went to Brussels without stopping.

At first sight Brussels seemed to be *en fête*, flags were waving from every window, Boy Scouts were everywhere looking very important, and the whole population seemed to be in the streets. Nearly every one wore little coloured flags or ribbons—a favourite badge was the Belgian colours with the English and French intertwined. It did not seem possible that war could be so near, and yet if one looked closer one saw that many of the flags giving such a gay appearance were Red Cross flags denoting that there an ambulance had been prepared for the wounded, and the Garde Civile in their picturesque uniform were constantly breaking up the huge crowds into smaller groups to avoid a demonstration.

The first thing to arrange was about the coming of my nurses, whether they were really needed and if so where they were to go. I heard from the authorities that it was highly probable that Brussels *would* be occupied by the Germans, and that it would be best to put off their coming, for a time at any rate. Private telegrams had long been stopped, but an official thought he might be able to get mine through, so I sent a long one asking that the nurses might not be sent till further notice. As a matter of fact it never arrived, and the next afternoon I heard that twenty-six nurses — instead of sixteen as was originally arranged — were already on their way. There were 15,000 beds in Brussels prepared for the reception of the wounded, and though there were not many wounded in the city just then, the nurses would certainly all be wanted soon if any of the

The Beginning of it All

rumours were true that we heard on all sides, of heavy fighting in the neighbourhood, and severe losses inflicted on the gallant little Belgian Army.

It was impossible to arrange for the nurses to go straight to their work on arrival, so it was decided that they should go to a hotel for one night and be drafted to their various posts the next day. Anyhow, they could not arrive till the evening, so in the afternoon I went out to the barriers to see what resistance had been made against the possible German occupation of Brussels. It did not look very formidable—some barbed-wire entanglements, a great many stones lying about, and the Gardes Civiles in their quaint old-fashioned costume guarding various points. That was all.

In due time my large family arrived and were installed at the hotel. Then we heard, officially, that the Germans were quite near the city, and that probably the train the nurses had come by would be the last to get through, and this proved to be the case. *Affiches* were pasted everywhere on the walls with the Burgomaster's message to his people :

Field Hospital & Flying Column

A Sad Hour! The Germans are at our Gates!

PROCLAMATION OF THE BURGOMASTER OF BRUSSELS

Citizens,—In spite of the heroic resistance of our troops, seconded by the Allied Armies, it is to be feared that the enemy may invade Brussels.

If this eventuality should take place, I hope that I may be able to count on the calmness and steadiness of the population.

Let every one keep himself free from terror—free from panic.

The Communal Authorities will not desert their posts. They will continue to exercise their functions with that firmness of purpose that you have the right to demand from them under such grave circumstances.

'I need hardly remind my fellow-citizens of their duty to their country. The laws of war forbid the enemy to force the population to give information as to the National Army and its method of defence. The inhabitants of Brussels must know that they are within their rights in refusing to give any information on this point to the invader. This refusal is their duty in the interests of their country.

Let none of you act as a guide to the enemy.

Let every one take precautions against spies and foreign agents, who will try to gather information or provoke manifestations.

The enemy cannot legitimately harm the family

The Beginning of it All

honour nor the life of the citizens, nor their private property, nor their philosophic or religious convictions, nor interfere with their religious services.

Any abuse committed by the invader must be immediately reported to me.

As long as I have life and liberty, I shall protect with all my might the dignity and rights of my fellow-citizens. I beg the inhabitants to facilitate my task by abstaining from all acts of hostility, all employment of arms, and by refraining from intervention in battles or encounters.

Citizens, whatever happens, listen to the voice of your Burgomaster and maintain your confidence in him; he will not betray it.

Long live Belgium free and independent!
Long live Brussels!

ADOLPHE MAX.

All that night refugees from Louvain and Termonde poured in a steady stream into Brussels, seeking safety. I have never seen a more pitiful sight. Little groups of terror-stricken peasants fleeing from their homes, some on foot, some more fortunate ones with their bits of furniture in a rough cart drawn by a skeleton horse or a large dog. All had babies, aged parents, or invalids with them. I realized then for the first time what war meant. We do not know in England. God grant we never may. It was not merely

Field Hospital & Flying Column

rival armies fighting battles, it was civilians —men, women, and children—losing their homes, their possessions, their country, even their lives. This invasion of unfortunates seemed to wake Brussels up to the fact that the German army was indeed at her gate. Hordes of people rushed to the Gare du Nord in the early dawn to find it entirely closed, no trains either entering or leaving it. It was said that as much rolling-stock as was possible had been sent to France to prevent it being taken by the Germans. There was then a stampede to the Gare du Midi, from whence a few trains were still leaving the city crammed to their utmost capacity.

In the middle of the morning I got a telephone message from the Belgian Red Cross that the Germans were at the barriers, and would probably occupy Brussels in half an hour, and that all my nurses must be in their respective posts before that time.

Oh dear, what a stampede it was. I told the nurses they must leave their luggage for the present and be ready in five minutes, and in less than that time we left the hotel, looking more like a set of rag-and-bone men than respectable British nursing sisters. One

The Beginning of it All

had seized a large portmanteau, another a bundle of clean aprons, another soap and toilet articles; yet another provident soul had a tea-basket. I am glad that the funny side of it did not strike me then, but in the middle of the next night I had helpless hysterics at the thought of the spectacle we must have presented. Mercifully no one took much notice of us—the streets were crowded and we had difficulty in getting on in some places—just at one corner there was a little cheer and a cry of " Vive les Anglais ! "

It took a long time before my flock was entirely disposed of. It had been arranged that several of them should work at one of the large hospitals in Brussels where 150 beds had been set apart for the wounded, five in another hospital at the end of the city, two in an ambulance station in the centre of Brussels, nine were taken over to a large fire-station that was converted into a temporary hospital with 130 beds, and two had been promised for a private hospital outside the barriers. It was a work of time to get the last two to their destinations; the Germans had begun to come in by that time, and we had to wait two hours to cross a certain street that led to the hospital, as all traffic had been stopped while the enemy entered Brussels.

It was an imposing sight to watch the German troops ride in. The citizens of Brussels behaved magnificently, but what a bitter humiliation for them to undergo. How should we have borne it, I wonder, if it had been London? The streets were crowded, but there was hardly a sound to be heard, and the Germans took possession of Brussels in silence. First the Uhlans rode in, then other cavalry, then the artillery and infantry. The latter were dog-weary, dusty and travel-stained—they had evidently done some forced marching. When the order was given to halt for a few minutes, many of them lay down in the street just as they were, resting against their packs, some too exhausted to eat, others eating sausages out of little paper bags (which, curiously enough, bore the name of a Dutch shop printed on the outside) washed down with draughts of beer which many of the inhabitants of Brussels, out of pity for their weary state, brought them from the little drinking-houses that line the Chaussée du Nord.

The Beginning of it All

The rear was brought up by Red Cross wagons and forage carts, commissariat wagons, and all the miscellaneous kit of an army on the march. It took thirty-six hours altogether for the army to march in and take possession. They installed themselves in the Palais de Justice and the Hôtel de Ville, having requisitioned beds, food and everything that they wanted from the various hotels. Poor Madame of the Hotel X. wept and wrung her hands over the loss of her beautiful beds. Alas, poor Madame! The next day her husband was shot as a spy, and she cared no longer about the beds.

In the meantime, just as it got dark, I installed my last two nurses in the little ambulance out beyond the barriers.

II

CHARLEROI AND ROUND ABOUT

THE Germans had asked for three days to pass through the city of Brussels; a week had passed and they showed no signs of going. The first few days more and more German soldiers poured in—dirty, footsore, and for the most part utterly worn out. At first the people of Brussels treated them with almost unnecessary kindness—buying them cake and chocolate, treating them to beer, and inviting them into their houses to rest—but by the end of the week these civilities ceased.

Tales of the German atrocities began to creep in—stories of Liège and Louvain were circulated from mouth to mouth, and doubtless lost nothing by being repeated.

There was no *real* news at all. Think how cut off we were—certainly it was nothing in comparison with what it was afterwards—

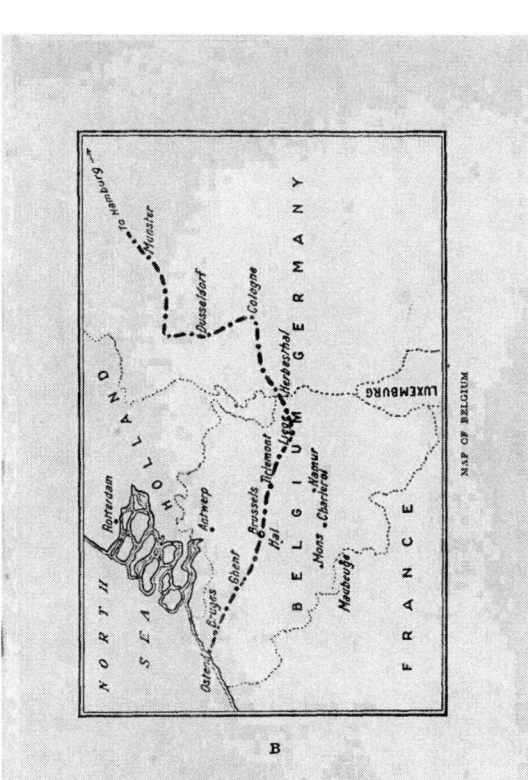

MAP OF BELGIUM

Charleroi & Round About

but we could not know that then—and anyway we learnt to accommodate ourselves to the lack of news by degrees. Imagine a Continental capital suddenly without newspapers, without trains, telephones, telegraphs; all that we had considered up to now essentials of civilized life. Personally, I heard a good deal of Belgian news, one way and another, as I visited all my flock each day in their various hospitals and ambulances stationed in every part of the city.

The hospital that we had to improvise at the fire-station was one of the most interesting pieces of work we had to do in Brussels. There were 130 beds altogether in six large wards, and the Sisters had to sleep at first in one, later in two large dormitories belonging to firemen absent on active service. The firemen who were left did all the cooking necessary for the nursing staff and patients, and were the most charming of men, leaving nothing undone that could augment the Sisters' comfort.

It is a great strain on temper and endurance for women to work and sleep and eat together in such close quarters, and on

Field Hospital & Flying Column

the whole they stood the test well. In a very few days the fire-station was transformed into a hospital, and one could tell the Sisters with truth that the wards looked *almost* like English ones. Alas and alas! At the end of the week the Germans put in eighty soldiers with sore feet, who had overmarched, and the glorious vision of nursing Tommy Atkins at the front faded into the prosaic reality of putting hundreds of cold compresses on German feet, that they might be ready all the sooner to go out and kill our men. War is a queer thing!!

* * * * *

On the following Tuesday afternoon the Burgomaster of Charleroi came into Brussels in an automobile asking for nurses and bringing with him a permit for this purpose from the German authorities. Charleroi, which was now also in German hands, was in a terrible state, and most of the city burnt down to the ground. It was crammed with wounded—both French and German—every warehouse and cottage almost were full of them, and they were very short of trained people.

The Central Red Cross Bureau sent a

Charleroi & Round About

message, asking if three of us would go back with him. *Would we!* Was it not the chance we had been longing for. In ten minutes Sister Elsie, Sister Grace and I were in that automobile speeding to Charleroi. I had packed quickly into a portmanteau all I thought I was likely to want in the way of uniform and other clothing, with a few medical comforts for the men, and a little tea and cocoa for ourselves. The two Sisters had done likewise—so we were rather horrified when we got to Hal, where we had to change automobiles, the Burgomaster said he could not possibly take any of our luggage, as we must get into quite a small car—the big one having to return to Brussels. He assured us that our things would be sent on in a few days—so back to Brussels went my portmanteau with all my clean aprons and caps and everything else, and I did not see it again for nearly a week. But such is war!

We waited nearly an hour at Hal while our German permits were examined, and then went off in the small car. It was heart-breaking to see the scenes of desolation as we passed along the road. Jumet—the working-class suburb of Charleroi—was entirely burnt down, there did not seem to be one house left intact. It is indeed terrible when historic and consecrated buildings such as those at Louvain and Rheims are burnt down, but in a way it is more pathetic to see these poor little cottages destroyed, that must have meant so much to their owners, and it makes one's heart ache to see among the crumbling ruins the remains of a baby's perambulator, or the half-burnt wires of an old four-post bed. Probably the inhabitants of Jumet had all fled, as there was no one to be seen as we went through the deserted village, except some German sentries pacing up and down.

Parts of Charleroi were still burning as we got to it, and a terrible acrid smoke pervaded everything. Here the poorer streets were spared, and it was chiefly the rich shops and banks and private houses that had been destroyed. Charleroi was the great Birmingham of Belgium—coal-pits all round, with many great iron and steel works, now of course all idle, and most of the owners entirely ruined. The town was absolutely crammed with German troops as we passed through; it had now been occupied for two

Charleroi & Round About

or three days and was being used as a great military depot.

But Charleroi was not to be our final destination—we went on a few more kilometres along the Beaumont road, and drew up at a fairly large building right out in the country. It was a hospital that had been three parts built ten years ago, then abandoned for some reason and never finished. Now it was being hastily fitted up as a Red Cross hospital, and stretcher after stretcher of wounded—both French and German—were being brought in as we arrived.

The confusion that reigned within was indescribable. There were some girls there who had attended first-aid lectures, and they were doing their best; but there were no trained nurses and no one particularly in command. The German doctor had already gone, one of the Belgian doctors was still working there, but he was absolutely worn out and went off before long, as he had still cases to attend to in the town before he went to his well-earned bed. He carried off the two Sisters with him, till the morning, and I was left alone with two or three Red Cross damsels to face the night. It is a dreadful nightmare to look back at. Blood-stained uniforms hastily cut off the soldiers were lying on the floor—half-open packets of dressings were on every locker; basins of dirty water or disinfectant had not been emptied; men were moaning with pain, calling for water, begging that their dressings might be done again; and several new cases just brought in were requiring urgent attention. And the cannon never ceased booming. I was not accustomed to it then, and each crash meant to me rows of men mown down — maimed or killed. I soon learnt that comparatively few shells do any damage, otherwise there would soon be no men left at all. In time, too, one gets so accustomed to cannon that one hardly hears it, but I had not arrived at that stage then: this was my baptism of fire.

Among the other miseries of that night was the dreadful shortage of all hospital supplies, and the scarcity of food for the men. There was a little coffee which they would have liked, but there was no possibility of hot water. The place had been hastily fitted up with electric light, and the kitchen was arranged for steam cooking, so there was not even a gas-jet to heat anything on. I had a spirit-lamp and methylated spirit in my portmanteau, but, as I said, my luggage had been all wafted away at Hal.

But the night wore away somehow, and with the morning light came plans of organization and one saw how things could be improved in many ways, and the patients made more comfortable. The hospital was a place of great possibilities in some ways; its position standing almost at the top of a high hill in its own large garden was ideal, and the air was gloriously bracing, but little of it reached the poor patients as unfortunately the Germans had issued a proclamation forbidding any windows to be open, in case, it was said, anyone should fire from them—and as we were all prisoners in their hands, we had to do as we were bid.

At nine o'clock the Belgian doctor and the German commandant appeared, and I went off with the former to help with an amputation of arm, in one of the little temporary ambulances in the town of M——, three kilometres away. The building had been a little dark shop and not very convenient, and if the patient had not been so desperately ill, he would have been moved to Charleroi for his operation. He was a French tirailleur—a lad about twenty, his right arm had been severely injured by shrapnel several days before, and was gangrenous right up to the shoulder. He was unconscious and moaning slightly at intervals, but he stood the operation very well, and we left him fairly comfortable when we had to return to the hospital.

We got back about twelve, which is the hour usually dedicated to patients' dinner, but it was impossible to find anything to eat except potatoes. We sent everywhere to get some meat, but without success, though in a day or two we got some kind of dark meat which I thought must be horse. (Now from better acquaintance with ancient charger, I know it to have been so.) There was just a little milk that was reserved for the illest patients, no butter or bread. I was beginning to feel rather in need of food myself by that time. There had been, of course, up to then no time to bother about my own meals, and I had had nothing since breakfast the day before, that is about thirty hours ago, except a cup of coffee which I had begged from the concierge before starting with the doctor for the amputation case.

Well, there was nothing to eat and only the dirtiest old woman in all the world to cook it, but at three o'clock we managed to serve the patients with an elegant dish of underdone lentils for the first course, and overdone potatoes for the second, and partook ourselves gratefully thereof, after they had finished. In the afternoon of that day a meeting of the Red Cross Committee was held at the hospital, and I was sent for and formally installed as Matron of the hospital with full authority to make any improvements I thought necessary, and with the stipulation that I might have two or three days' leave every few weeks, to go and visit my scattered flock in Brussels. The appointment had to be made subject to the approval of the German commandant, but apparently he made no objection—at any rate I never heard of any.

And then began a very happy time for me, in spite of many difficulties and disappointments. I can never tell the goodness of the Committee and the Belgian doctor to me, and their kindness in letting me introduce all our pernickety English ways to which they were not accustomed, won my gratitude for ever. Never were Sisters so loyal and unselfish as mine. The first part of the time they were overworked and underfed, and no word of grumbling or complaint was ever heard from them. They worked from morning till night and got the hospital into splendid order. The Committee were good enough to allow me to keep the best of the Red Cross workers as probationers and to forbid entrance to the others. We had suffered so much at their hands before this took place, that I was truly grateful for this permission as no discipline or order was possible with a large number of young girls constantly rushing in and out, sitting on patients' beds, meddling with dressings, and doing all kinds of things they shouldn't.

I am sure that no hospital ever had nicer patients than ours were. The French patients, though all severely wounded and prisoners in the hands of the Germans, bore their troubles cheerfully, even gaily. We had a great variety of regiments represented in the hospital: Tirailleurs, Zouaves, one Turco from Algeria—our big good-natured Adolphe—soldiers from Paris, from Brittany and from Normandy, especially from Calvados. The German soldiers, too, behaved quite well, and were very grateful for everything done for them—mercifully we had no officers. We had not separate rooms for them—French and German soldiers lay side by side in the public wards.

One of the most harrowing things during that time was the way all the Belgians were watching for the English troops to deliver them from the yoke of their oppressor. Every day, many times a day, when German rules got more and more stringent and autocratic, and fresh tales of unnecessary harshness and cruelty were circulated, they would say over and over again, "Where are the English? If only the English would come!" Later they got more bitter and we heard, "Why don't the English come and help us as they promised? If only the English would come, it would be all right." And so on, till I almost felt as if I could not bear it any longer. One morning some one came in and said English soldiers had been seen ten kilometres away. We heard the sound of distant cannon in a new direction, and watched and waited, hoping to see the English ride in. But some one must have mistaken the German khaki for ours, for no English were ever near that place. There was no news of what was really happening in the country, no newspapers ever got through, and we had nothing to go upon but the German *affiches* proclaiming victories everywhere, the German trains garlanded with laurels and faded roses, marked " Destination—Paris," and the large batches of French prisoners that were constantly marched through the town. An inscription written over a doorway in Charleroi amused us rather : " Vive Guillaume II, roi de l'univers." Not yet, not yet, William.

Later on the Belgians issued a wonderful little newspaper at irregular intervals of three or four days, typewritten and passed from hand to hand. The most amazing news was published in it, which we always firmly believed, till it was contradicted in the next issue. I collected two or three copies of this paper as a curiosity, but unfortunity lost them later on, with all my papers and luggage. One or two items I remember quite well. One gave a vivid account of how the Queen of Holland had killed her husband because he had allowed the Germans to pass through Maestricht; another even more circumstantial story was that England had declared war on Holland, Holland had submitted at once, and England imposed many stringent conditions, of which I only remember two. One was, that all her trade with Germany should cease at once; secondly, that none of her lighthouses should show light at night.

One of the German surgeons who used to operate at our hospital was particularly ingenious in inventing tortures for me; I used to have to help him in his operations, and he would recount to me with gusto how the English had retreated from Mons, how the Germans were getting nearer and nearer to Paris, how many English killed, wounded and prisoners there were, and so on. One morning he began about the Fleet and said that a great battle was going on in the North Sea, and going very badly for the English. I had two brothers fighting in the North Sea of whom I had no news since the war began, and I could bear it no longer, but fled from the operating-room.

Charleroi and its neighbourhood was just one large German camp, its position on the railway making it a particularly valuable base for them. The proclamations and rules for the behaviour of the inhabitants became daily more and more intolerant. It was forbidden to lock the door, or open the window, or pull down the blinds, or allow your dog out of the house; all German officers were to be saluted—and if there was any doubt, any German soldier was to be saluted, and so on, day after day. One really funny one I wish I could reproduce. It forbade anyone to " wear a menacing look " but it did not say who was to be the judge of this look.

Every one was too restless and unhappy to settle to anything, all the most important shops were burnt down, and very few of those that were left were open. The whole population seemed to spend all their time in the street waiting for something to happen. Certainly the Germans seem to have had a special " down " on Charleroi and its neighbourhood, so many villages in its vicinity were burnt down and most abominable cruelties practised on its inhabitants. The peasants who were left were simply terrorized, as no doubt the Germans meant them to be, and a white flag hung from nearly every cottage window denoting complete submission. In one village some German soldier wrote in chalk on the door of a house where he had been well received, "Güte Leute hier," and these poor people got chalk and tried to copy the difficult German writing on every door in the street. I am afraid that did not save them, however, when their turn came. It was the utter ruthlessness and foresight with which every contingency was prepared for that appalled me and made me realize what a powerful enemy we were up against. Everything was thought out down to the last detail and must have been prepared months beforehand. Even their wagons for transport were all painted the same slate-grey colour, while the English and Belgians were using any cart they could commandeer in the early days, as I afterwards saw in a German camp Pickford's vans and Lyons' tea carts that they had captured from us. Even their postal arrangements were complete; we saw their grey "Feld-Post" wagons going to and fro quite at the beginning of the war.

Several people in Charleroi told me that the absolute system and organization of destruction frightened them more than the actual fire itself. Every German soldier had a little hatchet, and when Charleroi was fired, they simply went down the street as if they had been drilled to it for months, cutting a square hole in the panel of each door, and throwing a ball of celluloid filled with benzine inside. This exploded and set the house on fire, and later on the soldiers would return to see if it was burning well. They were entirely indifferent as to whether anyone were inside or not, as the following incident, which came under my notice, will show. Two English Red Cross Sisters were working at an ambulance in Charleroi, and lodging with some people in the centre of the city. When the town was being burnt they asked leave to go and try to save some of their possessions. They arrived at the house, however, and found it entirely burnt down, and all their things destroyed. They were returning rather sorrowfully to their hospital

Charleroi & RoundAbout

when an old woman accosted them and told them that a woman with a new-born infant was lying in bed in one of the burning houses.

The house was not burning badly, and they got into it quite easily and found the woman lying in bed with her little infant beside her, almost out of her wits with terror, but too weak to move. The nurses found they could not manage alone, so went down into the street to find a man. They found, after some trouble, a man who had only one arm and got him to help them take the woman to the hospital. One of the nurses was carrying the baby, the other with the one-armed man was supporting the mother, when the German soldiers fired at the little party, and the one-armed man fell bleeding at the side of the road. The Sisters were obliged to leave him for the moment, and went on with the mother and infant to the hospital, got a stretcher and came back and fetched the man and brought him also to the hospital. It was only a flesh wound in the shoulder and he made a good recovery, but what a pitiful little group to waste ammunition on—a newly confined mother and her infant, two Red Cross Sisters and a crippled man.

One can only imagine that they were drunk when they did these kind of things, for individually the German soldier is generally a decent fellow, though some of the Prussian officers are unspeakable. Discipline is very severe and the soldiers are obliged to carry out orders without troubling themselves about rights and wrongs. It is curious that very few German soldiers know why they are fighting, and they are always told such wonderful stories of German victories that they think the war will soon be over. When they arrived at Charleroi, for instance, they were told they were at Charleville, and nearly all our wounded German soldiers thought they were already in France. They also thought Paris was already taken and London in flames. It hardly seems worth while to lie to them in this way, for they are bound to find out the truth sooner or later.

III

OUR HOSPITAL AND PATIENTS

AFTER we had had a long week of night and day work, two more of my nurses suddenly turned up at the hospital. They had most unexpectedly got a message that I had sent in by hand to Brussels, begging for nurses and saying how hard pressed we were, and had got permission to come out in a Red Cross motor-ambulance. I was, of course, delighted to see them, and with their help we soon settled down into the ordinary routine of hospital life, and forgot we were prisoners under strict supervision, having all kinds of tiresome rules and regulations to keep.

The question of supplies was a very difficult one from the first. We were short of everything, very short of dressings, chloroform and all kinds of medical supplies, and especially (even worse in one way) very short of hospital linen such as sheets and towels and shirts and drawers, and we had the greatest difficulty in getting anyone to come and wash for us. One might have thought that with almost every one out of work, there would have been no lack of women; but the hospital was a long way from the nearest town and I suppose they were afraid to come; also, of course, many, very many, had had their houses burnt, lost their all and fled away. The food question was a very difficult one also. We had to live just from day to day and be thankful for small mercies. Naturally for ourselves it would not have mattered at all, but it *did* matter very much for our poor patients, who were nearly all very ill. Meat was always difficult often impossible to get, and at first there was no bread, which, personally, I missed more than anything else; afterwards we got daily rations of this. Butter there was none; eggs and milk very scarce, only just enough for the very severely wounded. Potatoes and lentils we had in great quantities, and on that diet one would never starve, though it was not an ideal one for sick men.

I remember one morning when we had only

potatoes for the men's dinner; the cook had just peeled an immense bucket of them and was putting them on to boil when some German soldiers came and took the lot, and this so infuriated the cook that we had to wait hours before we could get another lot prepared and cooked for the patients' dinner. The water-supply was another of our difficulties. All the watercourses in the neighbourhood were polluted with dead bodies of men and horses and no water was fit to drink. There was a horrible, greenish, foul-smelling stream near the hospital, which I suppose eventually found its way into the river, and it sickened me to imagine what we were drinking, even though it was well boiled.

It was very hot weather and the men all dreadfully thirsty. There was one poor Breton soldier dying of septicæmia, who lay in a small room off the large ward. He used to shriek to every passer-by to give him drink, and no amount of water relieved his raging thirst. That voice calling incessantly night and day, "A boire, à boire!" haunted me long after he was dead. The taste of long-boiled water is flat and nasty, so we made weak decoctions of camomile-tea for the men, which they seemed to like very much. We let it cool, and kept a jug of it on each locker so that they could help themselves whenever they liked.

Some of the ladies of the town were very kind indeed in bringing in wine and little delicacies for our sick, and for ourselves, too, sometimes. We were very grateful to them for all their kindness in the midst of their own terrible trouble and anxieties.

All the first ten days the cannon boomed without ceasing; by degrees it got more distant, and we knew the forts of Maubeuge were being bombarded by the famous German howitzers, which used to shake the hospital to its foundations. The French soldiers in the wards soon taught us to distinguish the sounds of the different cannon. In a few days we knew as well as they did whether it was French or German artillery firing.

Our hospital was on the main Beaumont road, and in the midst of our work we would sometimes glance out and watch the enormous reinforcements of troops constantly being sent up. Once we saw a curious sight. Two large motor-omnibuses with "Leipziger lokal-anzeiger" painted on their

Our Hospital & Patients

side went past, each taking about twenty-five German Béguine nuns to the battlefield, the contrast between this very modern means of transport and the archaic appearance of the nuns in their mediæval dress was very striking.

Suddenly one Sunday morning the cannonading ceased—there was dead silence—Maubeuge was taken, and the German army passed on into France. It is difficult to explain the desolating effect when the cannon suddenly ceases. At first one fears and hates it, then one gets accustomed to it and one feels at least *something is being done*—there is still a chance. When it ceases altogether there is a sense of utter desertion, as if all hope had been given up.

* * * *

On the morning of September 1 the German commandant suddenly appeared in the wards at 7 o'clock, and said that all the German wounded were going to be sent off to Germany at once, and that wagons would be coming in an hour's time to take them to the station. We had several men who were not fit to travel, amongst them a soldier who had had his leg amputated only twelve

Field Hospital & Flying Column

hours before. I ought to have learnt by that time the futility of argument with a German official, but I pleaded very hard that a few of the men might be left till they were a little better able to stand the journey, for there is no nationality among wounded, and we could not bear even German patients to undergo unnecessary suffering. But my remonstrances were quite in vain, and one could not help wondering what would become of *our* wounded if the Germans treated their own so harshly. I heard from other ambulances that it was their experience as well as mine that the lightly wounded were very well looked after, but the severely wounded were often very inconsiderately treated. They were no longer any use as fighting machines and only fit for the scrap-heap. It is all part of the German system. They are out for one purpose only, that is to win—and they go forward with this one end in view—everything else, including the care of the wounded, is a side-issue and must be disregarded and sacrificed if necessary.

We prepared the men as well as we could for the long ride in the wagons that must precede the still longer train journey. Once

Our Hospital & Patients

on the ambulance-train, however, they would be well looked after; it was the jolting on the country road I feared for many of them. None of us were permitted to accompany them to Charleroi station, but the driver of one of the wagons told me afterwards that the man with the amputated leg had been taken out dead at the station, as he had had a severe hæmorrhage on the way, which none of his comrades knew how to treat. He also told us that all the big hospitals at Charleroi were evacuating their German wounded, and that he had seen two other men taken out of carts quite dead. We took this to mean very good news for us, thinking that the Germans must have had a severe reverse to be taking away their wounded in such a hurry. So we waited and hoped, but as usual nothing happened and there was no news.

We had a very joyful free sort of feeling at having got rid of the German patients. The French soldiers began to sing The Marseillaise as soon as they had gone, but we were obliged to stop them as we feared the German doctor or commandant, who were often prowling about, might hear. Losing so many patients made the work much lighter for the time being, and about this time, too, several of the severely wounded men died. They had suffered so frightfully that it was a great relief when they died and were at rest. The curé of the parish church was so good to them, never minding how many times a day he toiled up that long hill in the blazing sunshine, if he could comfort some poor soul, or speed them on their way fortified with the last rites of the Church.

One poor Breton soldier could not bear the thought of being buried without a coffin—he spoke about it for days before he died, till Madame D——, a lady living in the town to whom we owe countless acts of kindness, promised that she would provide a coffin, so the poor lad died quite happily and peacefully, and the coffin and a decent funeral were provided in due course, though, of course, he was not able to have a soldier's funeral. Some of these poor French soldiers were dreadfully homesick—most of them were married, and some were fathers of families who had to suddenly leave their peaceful occupations to come to the war. Jules, a dapper little pastrycook with pink cheeks and bright black eyes, had been making a batch of tarts when his summons had come. And he was much better suited to making tarts than to fighting, poor little man, for he was utterly unnerved by what he had gone through, and used to have dreadful fits of crying and sobbing which it was very difficult to stop.

Some of the others, and especially the Zouaves, one could not imagine in any other profession than that of soldiering. How jolly and cheerful they were, always making the best of everything, and when the German patients had gone we really had time to nurse them and look after them properly. Those who were able for the exertion were carried out to the garden, and used to lie under the pear-trees telling each other wonderful stories of what they had been through, and drinking in fresh health and strength every day from the beautiful breeze that we had on the very hottest days up on our hill. We had to guard them very carefully while they were in the garden, however, for if one man had tried to escape the hospital would have been burnt down and the officials probably shot. So two orderlies and two Red Cross probationers were always on duty there, and I think they enjoyed it as much as the men.

Suddenly a fresh thunderbolt fell.

One Sunday morning the announcement was made that every French patient was to go to Germany on Monday morning at eight.

We were absolutely in despair. We had one man actually dying, several others who must die before long, eight or ten who were very severely wounded in the thigh and quite unable to move, two at least who were paralysed, many who had not set foot out of bed and were not fit to travel—we had not forgotten the amputation case of a few days before, who was taken out dead at Charleroi station. I was so absolutely miserable about it that I persuaded the Belgian doctor to go to the commandant, and beg that the worst cases might be left to us, which he very pluckily did, but without the slightest effect—they must all go, ill or well, fit or unfit. After all the German patients were returning to their own country and people, but these poor French soldiers were going ill and wounded as prisoners to

Our Hospital & Patients

suffer and perhaps die in an enemy's country—an enemy who knew no mercy.

I could hardly bear to go into the wards at all that day, and busied myself with seeing about their clothes. Here was a practical illustration of the difference in equipment between the German and French soldiers. The German soldiers came in well equipped, with money in their pockets and all they needed with them. Their organization was perfect, and they were prepared for the war; the French were not. When they arrived at the hospital their clothes had been cut off them anyhow, with jagged rips and splits by the untrained Red Cross girls. Trained ambulance workers are always taught to cut by the seam when possible. Many had come without a cap, some without a greatcoat, some without boots; all had to be got ready somehow. The hospital was desperately short of supplies—we simply could not give them all clean shirts and drawers as we longed to do. The trousers were our worst problem, hardly any of them were fit to put on. We had a few pairs of grey and black striped trousers, the kind a superior shopman might wear, but we were afraid to give those to the men as we thought the Germans would think they were going to try to escape if they appeared in civil trousers, and might punish them severely. So we mended up these remnants of French red pantaloons as best we could. One man we *had* to give civil trousers as he had only a few shreds of pantaloon left, and these he promised to carry in his hand to show that he really could not put them on.

The men were laughing and joking and teasing one another about their garments, but my heart was as heavy as lead. I simply could not *bear* to let the worst cases go. One or two of the Committee came up and we begged them to try what they could do with the commandant, but they said it was not the least use, and from what I had seen myself, I had to confess that I did not think it would be. The patient I was most unhappy about was a certain French count we had in the hospital. He had been shot through the back at the battle of Nalinnes, and was three days on the battlefield before he was picked up. Now he lay dying in a little side room off the ward. The least movement caused him acute agony, even the pillow had to be moved an inch at a time before it could be turned, and it took half an hour to change his shirt. The doctor had said in the morning he could not last another forty-eight hours. But if he was alive the next morning he would be put in those horrible springless carts, and jolted, jolted down to the station, taken out and transferred to a shaky, vibrating train, carrying him far away into Germany.

Mercifully he died very peacefully in his sleep that evening, and we were all very thankful that the end should have come a little earlier than was expected.

Late that night came a message that the men were not to start till midday, so we got them all dressed somehow by eleven. All had had bad nights, nearly all had temperatures, and they looked very poor things when they were dressed; even fat, jolly Adolphe looked pale and subdued. We had not attempted to do anything with the bad bed cases; if they *must* go they must just go wrapped up in their blankets. But we unexpectedly got a reprieve. A great German chief came round that morning, accompanied by the German doctor and German commandant, and gave the order that the very bad cases were to remain for the present. I I cannot say how thankful we were for this respite and so were the men. Poor Jules, who was very weak from pain and high temperature, turned to the wall and cried from pure relief.

At 11.30 the patients had their dinner— we tried to give them a good one for the last —and then every moment we expected the wagons to come. We waited and waited till at length we began to long for them to come and get the misery of it over. At last they arrived, and we packed our patients into it as comfortably as we could on the straw. Each had a parcel with a little money and a few delicacies our ever-generous Madame D—— had provided. It was terrible to think of some of these poor men in their shoddy uniforms, without an overcoat, going off to face a long German winter.

So we said good-bye with smiles and tears and thanks and salutations. And the springless wagons jolted away over the rough road, and fortunately we had our bad cases to occupy our thoughts. An order came to prepare at once for some more wounded who

Our Hospital & Patients

might be coming in at any time, so we started at once to get ready for any emergency. The beds were disinfected and made up with our last clean sheets and pillow-cases, and the wards scrubbed, when there was a shout from some one that they were bringing in wounded at the hospital gate. We looked out and true enough there were stretchers being brought in. I went along to the operating theatre to see that all was ready there in case of necessity, when I heard shrieks and howls of joy, and turned round and there were all our dear men back again, and they, as well as the entire staff, were half mad with delight. They were all so excited, talking at once, one could hardly make out what had happened; but at last I made one of them tell me quietly. It appeared that when the wagons got down to Charleroi station, the men were unloaded and put on stretchers, and were about to be carried into the station when an officer came and pointed a pistol at them (why, no one knew, for they were only obeying orders), and said they were to wait. So they waited there outside the station for a long time, guarded by a squad of German soldiers, and at last were told that the train to Germany was already full and that they must return to the hospital. They all had to be got back into bed (into our disinfected beds, with the last of the clean sheets!) and fed and their dressings done, and so on, and they were so excited that it took a long time before they could settle down for the night. But it was a very short reprieve, for the next day they had to go off again and there was no coming back this time.

I often think of those poor lads in Germany and wonder what has become of them, and if those far-off mothers all think their sons are dead. If so, what a joyful surprise some of them will have some day—after the war.

IV

THE RETURN TO BRUSSELS

THIS seemed a favourable moment for me to go to Brussels for a day or two to visit my flock. The Committee gave me leave to go, but begged me to be back in two days, which I promised to do. A *laissez-passer* had been obtained from the German commandant for a Red Cross automobile to go into Brussels to fetch some supplies of dressings and bandages of which all the hospitals in the neighbourhood were woefully short. And I was also graciously accorded a ticket of leave by the same august authority to go for two days, which might be extended to three according to the length of stay of the automobile.

The night before I left, an aeroplane which had been flying very high above the town dropped some papers. The doctor with whom I was lodging secured one and brought it back triumphantly. It contained a message from the Burgomaster of Antwerp to his fellow-citizens, and ended thus : " Courage, fellow-citizens, in a fortnight our country will be delivered from the enemy."

We were all absurdly cheered by this message, and felt that it was only a matter of a short time now before the Germans were driven out of Belgium. We had had no news for so long that we thought probably the Antwerp Burgomaster had information of which we knew nothing, and I was looking forward to hearing some good news when I got to Brussels.

I found Brussels very much changed since I had left it some weeks before. Then it was in a fever of excitement, now it was in the chill of dark despair. German rule was firmly established, and was growing daily more harsh and humiliating for its citizens. Everything was done to Germanize the city, military automobiles were always dashing through, their hooters playing the notes of the Emperor's salute, Belgian automobiles that had been requisitioned whirred up and down the streets filled with German officers' wives and children, German time was kept,

The Return to Brussels

German money was current coin, and every café and confectioner's shop was always crowded with German soldiers. Every day something new was forbidden. Now it was taking photographs—the next day no cyclist was allowed to ride, and any cyclist in civil dress might be shot at sight, and so on. The people were only *just* kept in hand by their splendid Burgomaster, M. Max, but more than once it was just touch and go whether he would be able to restrain them any longer.

What made the people almost more angry than anything else was the loss of their pigeons, as many of the Belgians are great pigeon fanciers and have very valuable birds. Another critical moment was when they were ordered to take down all the Belgian flags. Up to that time the Belgian flag, unlike every other town that the Germans had occupied, had floated bravely from nearly every house in Brussels. M. Max had issued a proclamation encouraging the use of it early in the war. Now this was forbidden as it was considered an insult to the Germans. Even the Red Cross flag was forbidden except on the German military hospitals, and I thought Brussels looked indeed a melancholy city as we came in from Charleroi that morning in torrents of rain in the Red Cross car.

My first business was to go round and visit all my nurses. I found most of them very unhappy because they had no work. All the patients had been removed from the fire-station hospital and nearly all the private hospitals and ambulances were empty too. It was said that Germans would rather have all their wounded die than be looked after by Englishwomen, and there were dreadful stories afloat which I cannot think any German believed, of English nurses putting out the eyes of the German wounded. Altogether there were a good many English Sisters and doctors in Brussels—three contingents sent out by the Order of St. John of Jerusalem, to which we belonged, a large unit sent by the British Red Cross Society, and a good many sent out privately. It certainly was not worth while for more than a hundred English nurses to remain idle in Brussels, and the only thing to do now was to get them back to England as soon as possible. In the meantime a few of them took the law into their own hands, and slipped

The Return to Brussels

away without a passport, and got back to England safely by unofficial means.

The second afternoon I was in Brussels I received a note from one of my nurses who had been sent to Tirlemont in my absence by the Belgian Red Cross Society. The contents of the note made me very anxious about her, and I determined to go and see her if possible. I had some Belgian acquaintances who had come from that direction a few days before, and I went to ask their advice as to how I should set about it. They told me the best way, though rather the longest, was to go first to Mâlines and then on to Tirlemont from there, and the only possible way of getting there was to walk, as they had done a few days previously, and trust to getting lifts in carts. There had been no fighting going on when they had passed, and they thought I should get through all right.

So I set out very early in the morning accompanied by another Sister, carrying a little basket with things for one or two nights. I did not ask for any *laissez-passer*, knowing well enough that it would not be granted. We were lucky enough to get a tram the first part of the way, laden with peasants who had been in to Brussels to sell country produce to the German army, and then we set out on our long walk. It was a lovely late September morning, and the country looked so peaceful one could hardly believe that a devastating war was going on. Our way led first through a park, then through a high-banked lane all blue with scabious, and then at last we got on to a main road, when the owner of a potato cart crawling slowly along, most kindly gave us a long lift on our way.

We then walked straight along the Mâlines road, and I was just remarking to my companion that it was odd we should not have met a single German soldier, when we came into a village that was certainly full of them. It was about 11 o'clock and apparently their dinner hour, for they were all hurrying out of a door with cans full of appetizing stew in their hands. They took no notice of us and we walked on, but very soon came to a sandy piece of ground where a good many soldiers were entrenched and where others were busily putting up barbed-wire entanglements. They looked at us rather curiously

The Return to Brussels

but did not stop us, and we went on. Suddenly we came to a village where a hot skirmish was going on, two Belgian and German outposts had met. Some mitrailleuses were there in the field beside us, and the sound of rifle fire was crackling in the still autumn air. There was nothing to do but to go forward, so we went on through the village, and presently saw four German soldiers running up the street. It is not a pretty sight to see men running away. These men were livid with terror and gasping with deep breaths as they ran. One almost brushed against me as he passed, and then stopped for a moment, and I thought he was going to shoot us. But in a minute they went on towards the barbed-wire barricades and we made our way up the village street. Bullets were whistling past now, and every one was closing their shops and putting up their shutters. Several people were taking refuge behind a manure heap, and we went to join them, but the proprietor came out and said we must not stay there as it was dangerous for him. He advised us to go to the hotel, so we went along the street until we reached it, but it was not a very pleasant walk, as bullets were flying freely and the mitrailleuse never stopped going pom-pom-pom.

We found the hotel closed when we got to it, and the people absolutely refused to let us come in, so we stood in the road for a few minutes, not knowing which way to go. Then a Red Cross doctor saw us, and came and told us to get under cover at once. We explained that we desired nothing better, but that the hotel was shut, so he very kindly took us to a convent near by. It was a convent of French nuns who had been expelled from France and come to settle in this little village, and when they heard who we were they were perfectly charming to us, bringing beautiful pears from their garden and offering to keep us for the night. We could not do that, however, it might have brought trouble on them; but we rested half an hour and then made up our minds to return to Brussels. We could not go forward as the Mâlines road was blocked with soldiers, and we were afraid we could not get back the way we had come, past the barbed-wire barricades, but the nuns told us of a little lane at the back of their convent which led to the high road to Brussels, about fifteen miles distant.

The Return to Brussels

We went down this lane for about an hour, and then came to a road where four roads met, just as the nuns had said. I did not know which road to take, so asked a woman working outside the farm. She spoke Flemish, of which I only know a few words, and either I misunderstood her, or she thought we were German Sisters, for she pointed to another lane at the left which we had not noticed, and we thought it was another short cut to Brussels.

We had only gone a few yards down this lane when we met a German sentry who said "Halt!" We were so accustomed to them that we did not take much notice, and I just showed my Red Cross brassard as I had been accustomed to do in Charleroi when stopped. This had the German eagle stamped on it as well as the Belgian Red Cross stamp. The man saluted and let us pass. *Now* I realize that he too thought we were German Sisters.

We went on calmly down the lane and in two minutes we fell into a whole German camp. There were tents and wagons and cannon and camp fires, and thousands of soldiers. I saw some carts there which they must have captured from the English bearing the familiar names of "Lyons' Tea" and "Pickford" vans! An officer came up and asked in German what we wanted. I replied in French that we were two Sisters on our way to Brussels. Fortunately I could produce my Belgian Carte d'Identité, which had also been stamped with the German stamp. The only hope was to let him think we were Belgians. Had they known we were English I don't think anything would have saved us from being shot as spies. The officer had us searched, but found nothing contraband on us and let us go, though he did not seem quite satisfied. He really thought he had found something suspicious when he spied in my basket a small metal case. It contained nothing more compromising, however, than a piece of Vinolia soap. We had not the least idea which way to go when we were released, and went wrong first, and had to come back through that horrible camp again. Seven times we were stopped and searched, and each time I pointed to my German brassard and produced my Belgian Carte d'Identité. Sister did not speak French or German, but she was very good and did

The Return to Brussels

not lose her head, or give us away by speaking English to me. And at last—it seemed hours to us—we got safely past the last sentry. Footsore and weary, but very thankful, we trudged back to Brussels.

But that was not quite the end of our adventure, for just as we were getting into Brussels an officer galloped after us, and dismounted as soon as he got near us. He began asking in broken French the most searching questions as to our movements. I could not keep it up and had to tell him that we were English. He really nearly fell down with surprise, and wanted to know, naturally enough, what we were doing there. I told him the exact truth—how we had started out for Mâlines, were unable to get there and so were returning to Brussels. "But," he said at once, "you are not on the Mâlines road." He had us there, but I explained that we had rested at a convent and that the nuns had shown us a short cut, and that we had got on to the wrong road quite by mistake. He asked a thousand questions, and wanted the whole history of our lives from babyhood up. Eventually I satisfied him apparently, for he saluted, and said in

English as good as mine, " Truly the English are a wonderful nation," mounted his horse and rode away.

I did not try any more excursions to Tirlemont after that, but heard later on that my nurse was safe and in good hands.

* * * * *

My business in Brussels was now finished, and I wanted to return to my hospital at M. The German authorities met my request with a blank refusal. I was not at all prepared for this. I had only come in for two days and had left all my luggage behind me. Also one cannot leave one's hospital in this kind of way without a word of explanation to anyone. I could not go without permission, and it was more than sixty kilometres, too far to walk. I kept on asking, and waited and waited, hoping from day to day to get permission to return.

Instead of that came an order that every private ambulance and hospital in Brussels was to be closed at once, and that no wounded at all were to be nursed by the English Sisters. The doctor and several of the Sisters belonging to the Red Cross unit were imprisoned for twenty-four hours under

The Return to Brussels

suspicion of being spies. Things could not go on like this much longer. What I wanted to do was to send all my nurses back to England if it could be arranged, and return myself to my work at M. till it was finished. We were certainly not wanted in Brussels. The morning that the edict to close the hospitals had been issued, I saw about 200 German Red Cross Sisters arriving at the Gare du Nord.

I am a member of the International Council of Nurses, and our last big congress was held in Germany. I thus became acquainted with a good many of the German Sisters, and wondered what the etiquette would be if I should meet some of them now in Brussels. But I never saw any I knew.

After the Red Cross doctor with his Sisters had been released, he went to the German authorities and asked in the name of us all what they proposed doing with us. As they would no longer allow us to follow our profession, we could not remain in Brussels. The answer was rather surprising as they said they intended sending the whole lot of us to Liège. That was not pleasant news. Liège was rather uncomfortably near

Germany, and as we were not being sent to work there it sounded remarkably like being imprisoned. Every one who could exerted themselves on our behalf; the American Consul in particular went over and over again to vainly try to get the commandant to change his mind. We were to start on Monday morning, and on Sunday at midday the order still stood. But at four o'clock that afternoon we got a message to say that our gracious masters had changed our sentence, and that we were to go to England when it suited their pleasure to send us. But this did not suit *my* pleasure at all. Twenty-six nurses had been entrusted to my care by the St. John's Committee, four were still at M., and one at Tirlemont, and I did not mean to quit Belgian soil if I could help it, leaving five of them behind. So I took everything very quietly, meaning to stay behind at the last minute, and change into civilian dress, which I took care to provide myself with.

Then began a long period of waiting. Not one of my nurses was working, though there were a great many wounded in Brussels, and we knew that they were short-handed. There

The Return to Brussels

was nothing to do but to walk about the streets and read the new *affiches*, or proclamations, which were put up almost every day, one side in French, the other side in German, so that all who listed might read. They were of two kinds. One purported to give the news, which was invariably of important German successes and victories. The other kind were orders and instructions for the behaviour of the inhabitants of Brussels. It was possible at that time to buy small penny reprints of all the proclamations issued since the German occupation. They were not sold openly as the Germans were said to forbid their sale, but after all they could hardly punish people for reissuing what they themselves had published. Unfortunately I afterwards lost my little books of proclamations, but can reproduce a translation of a characteristic one that oppeared on October 5. The italics are mine.

BRUSSELS: October 5, 1914.

During the evening of September 25 the railway line and the telegraph wires were destroyed on the line Lovenjoul-Vertryck. In consequence of this, these two places have had to render an account of this, and had to give hostages on the morning of September 30.

Field Hospital & Flying Column

In future, the localities nearest to the place where similar acts take place *will be punished without pity—it matters little whether the inhabitants are guilty or not.* For this purpose hostages have been taken from all localities near the railway line thus menaced, and at the first attempt to destroy either the railway line or telephone or telegraph, *the hostages will be immediately shot.* Further, all the troops charged with the duty of guarding the railway have been ordered *to shoot any person with a suspicious manner* who approaches the line or telegraph or telephone wires.

VON DER GOLST.

And Von der Golst was recalled from Brussels later on because he was too lenient!

There is no reparation the Germans can ever make for iniquities of this kind—and they cannot deny these things as they have others, for they stand condemned out of their own mouths. Their own proclamations are quite enough evidence to judge them on.

One cannot help wondering what the German standard of right and wrong really is, because their private acts as well as their public ones have been so unworthy of a great nation. Some Belgian acquaintances of mine who had a large chateau in the country told me that such stealing among

The Return to Brussels

officers as took place was unheard of in any war before between civilized countries. The men had little opportunity of doing so, but the officers sent whole wagon-loads of things back to Germany with their name on. My friends said naturally they expected them to take food and wine and even a change of clothing, but in their own home the German officers quartered there had taken the very carpets off the floor and the chandeliers from the ceiling, and old carved cupboards that had been in the family for generations, and sent them back to Germany. They all begged me to make these facts public when I got back to England. Writing letters was useless as they never got through. Other Belgian friends told me of the theft of silver, jewellery, and even women's undergarments.

It was not etiquette in Brussels to watch the Germans, and particularly the officers. One could not speak about them in public, spies were everywhere, and one would be arrested at once at the first indiscreet word—but no one could be forced to look at them—and the habit was to ignore them altogether, to avert one's head, or shut one's eyes, or in extreme cases to turn one's back on them, and this hurt their feelings more than anything else could do. They *could* not believe apparently that Belgian women did not enjoy the sight of a beautiful officer in full dress—as much as German women would do.

All English papers were very strictly forbidden, but a few got in nevertheless by runners from Ostend. At the beginning of the German occupation the *Times* could be obtained for a franc. Later it rose to 3 francs then 5, then 9, then 15 francs. Then with a sudden leap it reached 23 francs on one day. That was the high-water mark, for it came down after that. The *Times* was too expensive for the likes of me. I used to content myself with the *Flandres Libérale*, a halfpenny paper published then in Ghent and sold in Brussels for a franc or more according to the difficulty in getting it in. These papers used to be wrapped up very tight and small and smuggled into Brussels in a basket of fruit or a cart full of dirty washing. They could not of course be bought in the shops, and the Germans kept a very keen look-out for them. We used to get them nevertheless almost every day in spite of them.

The mode of procedure was this: When it

The Return to Brussels

was getting dusk you sauntered out to take a turn in the fresh air. You strolled through a certain square where there were men selling picture post-cards, etc. You selected a likely looking man and went up and looked over his cards, saying under your breath "*Journal Anglais?*" or "*Flandres Libérale?*" which ever it happened to be. Generally you were right, but occasionally the man looked at you with a blank stare and you knew you had made a bad shot, and if perchance he had happened to be a spy, your lot would not have been a happy one. But usually you received a whispered "Oui, madame," in reply, and then you loudly asked the way to somewhere, and the man would conduct you up a side street, pointing the way with his finger. When no one was looking he slipped a tiny folded parcel into your hand, you slipped a coin into his, and the ceremony was over. But it was not safe to read your treasure at a front window or anywhere where you might be overlooked.

Sometimes these newspaper-sellers grew bold and transacted this business too openly and then there was trouble. One evening some of the nurses were at Benediction at the Carmelite Church, when a wretched newspaper lad rushed into the church and hid himself in a Confessional. He was followed by four or five German soldiers. They stopped the service and forbade any of the congregation to leave, and searched the church till they found the white and trembling boy, and dragged him off to his fate. We heard afterwards that a German spy had come up and asked him in French if he had a paper, and the boy was probably new at the game and fell into the trap.

About this time the Germans were particularly busy in Brussels. A great many new troops were brought in, amongst them several Austrian regiments and a great many naval officers and men. It was quite plain that some big undertaking was planned. Then one day we saw the famous heavy guns going out of the city along the Antwerp road. I had heard them last at Maubeuge, now I was to hear them again. Night and day reinforcements of soldiers poured into Brussels at the Gare du Nord, and poured out at the Antwerp Gate. No one whatever was permitted to pass to leave the city, the trams were all stopped at the barriers,

The Return to Brussels

and aeroplanes were constantly hovering above the city like huge birds of prey.

On Sunday, September 27, we woke to hear cannon booming and the house shaking with each concussion. The Germans had begun bombarding the forts which lay between Brussels and Antwerp. Looking from the heights of Brussels with a good glass, one could see shells bursting near Waelheim and Wavre St. Catherine. The Belgians were absolutely convinced that Antwerp was impregnable, and as we had heard that large masses of English troops had been landed there, we hoped very much that this would be the turning-point of the war, and that the Germans might be driven back out of the country.

On Wednesday, September 30, the sounds of cannon grew more distant, and we heard that Wavre St. Catherine had been taken. The Belgians were still confident, but it seems certain that the Germans were convinced that nothing could withstand their big guns, for they made every preparation to settle down in Brussels for the winter. They announced that from October 1 Brussels would be considered as part of German territory, and that they intended to re-establish the local postal service from that date. They reckoned without their host there, for the Brussels postmen refused to a man to take service under them, so the arrangement collapsed. They did re-establish postal communication between Brussels and Germany, and issued a special set of four stamps. They were the ordinary German stamps of 3, 5, 10 and 20 pfennig, and were surcharged in black " Belgien 3, 5, 10 and 20 centimes."

About this time, too, they took M. Max, the Burgomaster, off to Liège as prisoner, on the pretext that Brussels had not yet paid the enormous indemnity demanded of it. He held the people in the hollow of his hand, and the Brussels authorities very much feared a rising when he was taken off. But the Echevins, or College of Sheriffs, rose to the occasion, divided his work between them, and formed a local police composed of some of the most notable citizens of the town. They were on duty all day and night and divided the work into four-hour shifts, and did splendid work in warning the people against disorderly acts and preventing disturbances. It is not difficult to guess

The Return to Brussels

what would have happened if these patriotic citizens had not acted in this way—there would most certainly have been a rising among the people, and the German reprisals would have been terrible. As it was a German soldier who was swaggering alone down the Rue Basse was torn in pieces by the angry crowd, but for some reason this outbreak was hushed up by the German authorities.

V

A MEMORABLE JOURNEY

THE authorities seemed to be far too busy to trouble themselves about our affairs, and we could get no news as to what was going to happen to us. There was a good deal of typhoid fever in Brussels, and I thought I would employ this waiting time in getting inoculated against it, as I had not had time to do so before leaving England.

This operation was performed every Saturday by a doctor at the Hôpital St. Pierre, so on Saturday, October 3, I repaired there to take my turn with the others. The prick was nothing, and it never occurred to me that I should take badly, having had, I believe, typhoid when a child. But I soon began to feel waves of hot and cold, then a violent headache came on, and I was forced to go to bed with a very painful arm and a high temperature. I tossed about all night,

A Memorable Journey

and the next morning I was worse rather than better. At midday I received a message that every English Sister and doctor in Brussels was to leave for England the next day, via Holland, in a special train that had been chartered by some Americans and accompanied by the American Consul. How I rejoiced at my fever, for now I had a legitimate excuse for staying behind, for except at the point of the sword I did not mean to leave Belgium while I still had nurses there who might be in danger. The heads of all the various parties were requested to let their nurses know that they must be at the station the next day at 2 P.M. Several of my nurses were lodging in the house I was in, and I sent a message to them and to all the others that they must be ready at the appointed place and time. I also let a trusted few know that I did not mean to go myself, and gave them letters and messages for England.

The next morning I was still not able to get up, but several of my people came in to say good-bye to me in bed, and I wished them good luck and a safe passage back to England. By 1 P.M. they were all gone, and a great peace fell over the house. I struggled out of bed, put all traces of uniform away, and got out my civilian dress. I was no longer an official, but a private person out in Belgium on my own account, and intended to walk to Charleroi by short stages as soon as I was able. I returned to bed, and at five o'clock I was half asleep, half picturing my flock on their way to England, when there was a great clamour and clatter, and half a dozen of them burst into my room. They were all back once more!

They told me they had gone down to the station as they were told, and found the special train for Americans going off to the Dutch frontier. Their names were all read out, but they were not allowed to get into the train, and were told they were not going that day after all. The German officials present would give no reason for the change, and were extremely rude to the nurses. They told me my name had been read out amongst the others. They had been asked why I was not there, and had replied that I was ill in bed.

Just then a letter arrived marked "Urgent," and in it was an order that I

A Memorable Journey

should be at the station at 12 P.M. the next day *without fail*, accompanied by my nurses. I was very sad that they had discovered I did not want to go, because I knew now that they would leave no stone unturned to make me, but I determined to resist to the last moment and not go if I could help it. So I sent back a message to the Head Doctor of the Red Cross unit, asking him to convey to the German authorities the fact that I was ill in bed and could not travel the next day. Back came a message to say that they regretted to hear I was ill, and that I should be transferred at once to a German hospital and be attended by a German doctor. That, of course, was no good at all—I should then probably have been a German prisoner till the end of the war, and not have been the slightest use to anyone.

I very reluctantly gave in and said I would go. We were told that we should be safely conducted as far as the Dutch frontier, and so I determined to get across to Antwerp if I could from there and work my way back to Brussels in private clothes.

I scrambled up somehow the next day,

and found a very large party assembled outside the Gare du Nord, as every single English nurse and doctor in Brussels was to be expelled. There must have been fifteen or twenty doctors and dressers altogether, and more than a hundred Sisters and nurses.

A squad of German soldiers were lined up outside the station, and two officers guarded the entrance. They had a list of our names, and as each name was read out, we were passed into the station, where a long, black troop-train composed of third-class carriages was waiting for us. The front wagons were, I believe, full of either wounded or prisoners, as only a few carriages were reserved for us. However, we crowded in, eight of us in a carriage meant for six, and found, greatly to our surprise, that there were two soldiers with loaded rifles sitting at the window in each compartment. There was nothing to be said, we were entirely in their hands, and after all the Dutch frontier was not so very far off.

The soldiers had had orders to sit at the two windows and prevent us seeing out, but our two guards were exceedingly nice men, not

A Memorable Journey

Prussians but Danish Germans from Schleswig-Holstein, who did not at all enjoy the job they had been put to, so our windows were not shut nor our blinds down as those in some of the other carriages were.

A whistle sounded, and we were off. We went very very slowly, and waited an interminable time at each station. When evening came on we had only arrived as far as Louvain, and were interested to see two Zeppelins looming clear and black against the sunset sky, in the Mâlines direction flying towards Antwerp. It was not too dark to see the fearful destruction that had been dealt out to this famous Catholic University, only built and endowed during the last eighty years by great and heroic sacrifices on the part of both clergy and people. The two German soldiers in our carriage were themselves ashamed when they saw from the window the crumbling ruins and burnt-out buildings which are all that remain of Louvain now. One of them muttered: "If only the people had not fired at the soldiers, this would never have happened." Since he felt inclined to discuss the matter, one of us quoted the clause from The Hague

Convention of 1907 which was signed by Germany:

> The territory of neutral states is inviolable.
> The fact of a neutral Power resisting even by force, attempts to violate its neutrality cannot be regarded as a hostile act.

This was beyond him, but he reiterated: "No civilians have any right to fire at soldiers." And all the time they were killing civilians by bombs thrown on open cities. So deep has the sanctity of the army sunk into the German heart.

Night drew on, and one after another dropped into an uneasy sleep. But we were squeezed so tight, and the wooden third-class carriages were so hard, that it was almost more uncomfortable to be asleep than to be awake. We persuaded the two German soldiers to sit together as that made a little more room, and they soon went to sleep on each other's shoulders, their rifles between their knees. I was still feverish and seedy and could not sleep, but watched the beautiful starry sky, and meditated upon many things. We passed through Tirlemont, and I thought of my poor nurse

A Memorable Journey

there and wished I could get out and see what she was doing. Then I began to be rather puzzled by the way we were going. I knew this line pretty well, but could not make out where we were. About three o'clock in the morning I saw great forts on a hill sending out powerful search-lights. I knew I could not be mistaken, this must be Liège. And then we drew up in the great busy station, and I saw that it was indeed Liège. So we were on our way to Germany after all, and not to the Dutch frontier as we had been promised.

Next morning this was quite apparent, for we passed through Verviers and then Herbesthal the frontier town. At the latter place the doors of all our carriages were thrown violently open, and a Prussian officer shouted in a raucous voice "Heraus." Few of our party understood German, and they did not get out quickly enough to please his lordship, for he bellowed to the soldiers: "Push those women out of the train if they don't go quicker." Our things were thrown out after us as we scrambled out on to the platform, while two officers walked up and down having every bag and

Field Hospital & Flying Column

portmanteau turned out for their inspection. All scissors, surgical instruments and other useful articles were taken away from the Sisters, who protested in vain against this unfair treatment. The soldiers belonging to our carriage, seeing this, tumbled all our possessions back into the carriage, pretending that they had been examined—for we had become fast friends since we had shared our scanty stock of food and chocolate together. I was personally very thankful not to have my belongings looked at too closely, for I had several things I did not at all want to part with ; one was my camera, which was sewn up inside my travelling cushion, a little diary that I had kept in Belgium, and a sealed letter that had been given me as we stood outside the station at Brussels by a lady who implored me to take it to England and post it for her there, as it was to her husband in Petrograd, who had had no news of her since the war began. I had this in an inside secret pocket, and very much hoped I should get it through successfully.

We were ordered into the train again in the same polite manner that we had been

A Memorable Journey

ordered out. Our two soldiers were much upset by the treatment we had received. One had tears in his eyes when he told us how sorry he was, for he had the funny old-fashioned idea that Red Cross Sisters on active service should be treated with respect—even if they were English. He then told us that their orders were to accompany us to Cologne; he did not know what was going to happen to us after that. So Germany was to be our destination after all.

At the next station we stopped for a long time, and then the doors of the carriages were opened and we were each given a bowl of soup. It was very good and thick, and we christened it "hoosh" with remembrance of Scott's rib-sticking compound in the Antarctic; and there was plenty of it, so we providently filled up a travelling kettle with it for the evening meal. Then we went on again and crawled through that interminable day over the piece of line between Herbesthal and Cologne. Evening came, and we thought of the "hoosh," but when it came to the point no one could look at it, and we threw it out of the window. A horrible yellow scum had settled on the top of it and clung to the sides, so that it spoilt the kettle for making tea—and we *were* so thirsty.

At last, late at night, we saw the lights of Cologne. We had been thirty-two hours doing a journey that ordinarily takes six or seven. We were ordered out of the train when we reached the station, and were marched along between two rows of soldiers to a waiting-room. No porters were allowed to help us, so we trailed all along those underground corridors at Cologne station with our own luggage. Fortunately it was so late that there were not many people about. We were allowed to have a meal here, and could order anything we liked. Some coffee was a great comfort, and we were able to buy rolls and fruit for the journey.

An incident happened here that made my blood boil, but nothing could be done, so we had to set our teeth and bear it. A waiter came in smiling familiarly, with a bundle of papers under his arm, and put one of these illustrated weeklies beside each plate. On the front page was a horrible

A Memorable Journey

caricature of England—so grossly indecent that it makes me hot now even to think of it. As soon as I saw what they were, I went round to each place, gathered them up and put them aside.

As we waited I wondered what was to be the next step, and could not help thinking of my last visit to Cologne two years before. Then I went as a delegate to a very large Congress and Health Exhibition, when we were the honoured guests of the German National Council of Nurses. Then we were fêted by the Municipality of Cologne—given a reception at the Botanical Gardens, a free pass to all the sights of Cologne, a concert, tableaux, a banquet, I don't know what more. Now I was a prisoner heavily guarded, weary, dirty, humiliated in the very city that had done us so much honour.

After about three hours' wait we were ordered into another train, mercifully for our poor bones rather a more comfortable one this time, with plenty of room, and we went on our way, over the Rhine, looking back at Cologne Cathedral, on past Essen and Dusseldorf, into the very heart of Germany. It was rather an original idea

Field Hospital & Flying Column

—this trip through the enemy's country in the middle of the war!

In the morning we had a nice surprise. We arrived at Münster, and found breakfast awaiting us. The Red Cross ladies of that town kindly provide meals for all prisoners and wounded soldiers passing through. They seemed very surprised when all we English people turned up, but they were very kind in waiting on us, and after breakfast we got what was better than anything in the shape of a good wash. We had a long wait at Münster so there was no hurry, and we all got our turn under the stand-pipe and tap that stood in the station. Then on and on and on, and it seemed that we had always been in the train, till at last, late one evening, we arrived at Hamburg.

We were ordered out of the train here for a meal, and this was by far the most unpleasant time we had. Evidently the news of our arrival had preceded us, and a whole crowd of Hamburgers were at the station waiting to see us emerge from the train.

They were not allowed on to the platform, but lined the outside of the railing all the way down, laughing at us, spitting, hissing,

A Memorable Journey

jeering, and making insulting remarks. And though we were English we had to take it lying down. At the first indiscreet word from any of us they would have certainly taken off the men of our party to prison, though they would have probably done nothing more to us women than to delay our journey. There were about fifteen doctors and dressers with us, and we were naturally much more afraid for their safety than for our own. I think I shall never forget walking down that platform at Hamburg. We were hurried into a waiting-room, the door of which was guarded by two soldiers, and a meal of bread and cold meat ordered for us. The German waiters evidently much resented being asked to serve us, for they nearly threw the food at us.

Then something happened that made up for everything. A young German officer came up and asked in very good English if there was anything he could do for us in any way.

"I beg your pardon for speaking to you," he said, "but I received so much kindness from every one when I was in England, that it would be the greatest pleasure I

Field Hospital & Flying Column

could have if I could help you at all." And he started by giving the waiter the biggest blowing-up he had ever had in his life, for which I could have hugged him. He then went off and came back in a few minutes with fruit and chocolate and everything he could find for us to take with us. He was a very bright and shining star in a dark place. Then along the platform past that horrible, jeering crowd and into the train once more.

It was night, and most of us were asleep when the train stopped with a jerk, the doors of the train were thrown open, and the fresh, salty smell of the sea met our nostrils. Some of the party, hardly awake, thought they had to get out, and began to descend, but such volumes of wrath met their attempt that they hastily got in again. Every window in the train was shut, every blind pulled down and curtains closed, and a soldier with loaded rifle stood at each window. We were crossing the Kiel Canal. There were a great many people in England who would have given anything to have been in our shoes just then. But we saw absolutely nothing.

A Memorable Journey

They forgot to give us any breakfast that day, but we did not mind. Every mile now, along this flat, marshy country, was a mile nearer Denmark and freedom, and our spirits rose higher every moment. Though why the Germans should take us all through Germany and Denmark, when they could just as easily have dropped us on the Dutch frontier, I cannot even now imagine.

Early that afternoon we arrived at Vendrup, the Danish frontier, and the soldiers and the train that had brought us all the way from Cologne went back to Germany. It was difficult to realize that we were free once more, after two months of being prisoners with no news of home, tied down to a thousand tiresome regulations, and having witnessed terrible sights that none of us will ever forget. Strange and delightful it was to be able to send a telegram to England once more and to buy a paper; wonderful to see the friendly, smiling faces all round us. It felt almost like getting home again.

VI

A PEACEFUL INTERLUDE

LATE that night we arrived in Copenhagen. The kindness we received there surpasses all imagination. The Danish people opened their arms in welcome and gave us of their best with both hands. Every one went out of their way to be good to us, from the manager of the delightful Hotel Cosmopolite, where we were staying, to the utter strangers who sent us flowers, fruit, sweets, illustrated papers and invitations to every possible meal in such profusion.

Miss Jessen, the secretary of the Danish Council of Nurses, called at once and arranged a most delightful programme for every day of our stay in Copenhagen, bringing us invitations to see over the most important hospitals, and the Finsen Light Institute, the old Guildhall, the picture gallery, and anything else any of us wanted to see.

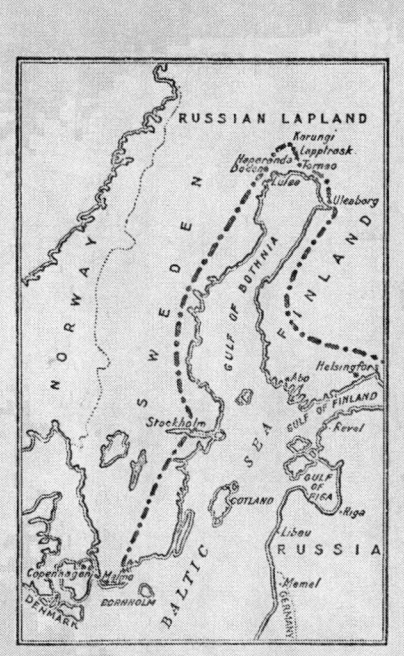

MAP OF OUR NORTHERN JOURNEY

A Peaceful Interlude

The president, Madame Tscherning, and the members of the same council, arranged a most delightful afternoon reception for us at the Palace Hotel, at which Dr. Norman Hansen welcomed us in the name of Denmark, and read us a poem which he had written in our honour.

TO THE BRITISH SURGEONS AND NURSES PASSING COPENHAGEN ON THEIR WAY FROM BELGIUM

Silent, we bid you welcome, in silence you answer'd our greeting
Because our lips must be closed, and your teeth are set
      Against the gale.
Our mouths are mute, our minds are open—
We shall greet you farewell in silence;
Sowers of good-will on fields where hate is sown—
    Fare ye well.

    C. NORMAN HANSEN, M.D.

That evening at dinner we all found a beautiful bunch of violets tied up with the Danish colours on our plates, and a pretty Danish medal with the inscription "Our God—our Land—our Honour" which had been issued to raise a fund for the Danish Red Cross Society. This was a little surprise for us on the part of the manager of the hotel, who, like every one else, simply overwhelmed us with kindness. One simply felt dreadfully ashamed of oneself for not having done more to deserve all this.

On the first day of our arrival in Denmark came the news of the downfall of Antwerp, and through all these delightful invitations and receptions there was a feeling in my heart that I was not free yet to enjoy myself. The downfall of Antwerp seemed almost like a personal loss. We had been so close to it, had shared our Belgian friends' hopes and fears, had watched the big German howitzers going out on the Antwerp road, had heard the bombardment of the forts, on our long journey through Belgium had seen the enormous reinforcements being sent up to take it. And now it had gone, and the Germans were marching on Ostend. What was the end of all this going to be? We *must* win in the end—but they are so strong and well organized—so *dreadfully* strong.

In that same paper I read an account from a Russian correspondent, telling of the distress in Poland, which they described as the "Belgium of Russia." It stated

A Peaceful Interlude

that the news just then was not good; the Germans were approaching Warsaw, and that the people in many of the villages were almost starving, as the Germans had eaten up almost everything. (How well I could believe that!) The paper went on to say that the troops were suffering severely from cholera and from typhoid fever and that there was a great scarcity of trained nurses. That gave me the clue for which I was unconsciously seeking—we had been turned out of Belgium, and now, perhaps, our work was to be in that other Belgium of Russia.

Three other Sisters wished to join me, and I telegraphed to St. John's to ask permission to offer our services to the Russian Red Cross. The answer was delayed, and as we could not go to Russia without permission from headquarters, we most reluctantly prepared to go back to England with all the others.

On the last morning our luggage, labelled Christiania-Bergen-Newcastle, had already gone down to the station when the expected telegram arrived: "You and three Sisters named may volunteer Russian Red Cross." We flew down to the station and by dint of many tips and great exertions we got our luggage out again. I should have been sorry to have lost my little all for the second time.

This permission to serve with the Russian Red Cross was confirmed later by a most kind letter from Sir Claude Macdonald, chairman of the St. John's Committee, so we felt quite happy about our enterprise.

We could not start for Russia for another ten days. We were to be inoculated against cholera for one thing, and then there were passports and visés to get and arrangements for the journey to be made. The ordinary route was by Abö, Stockholm and Helsingfors, but we were very strongly advised not to go this way, first, because of the possibility of mines in the Baltic, and, secondly, because a steamer, recently crossing that way, had been actually boarded, and some English people taken off by the Germans. And we had no desire to be caught a second time.

So it was decided to my great joy that we should travel all the way round by land, through Sweden, through a little bit of Lapland, just touching the Arctic Circle, through Finland and so to Petrograd. The thought of the places we had to go through thrilled me to the core—Karungi, Haparanda,

A Peaceful Interlude

Lapptrask, Tornea—the very names are as honey to the lips.

* * * * *

One might have expected that all the kindness and hospitality would cease on the departure of the majority of the party, but it was not so. Invitations of all kinds were showered on us. Lunches were the chief form of entertainment and very interesting and delightful they were. There was a lunch at the British Legation, one at the French Legation, one at the Belgian Legation where the minister was so pathetically glad of any crumbs of news of his beloved country; a delightful dinner to meet Prince Gustav of Denmark, an invitation to meet Princess Mary of Greece, another lunch with Madame Tscherning, the president of the Danish Council of Nurses, and the "Florence Nightingale of Denmark." Altogether we should have been thoroughly spoilt if it had lasted any longer! One of the most delightful invitations was to stay at Vidbek for the remainder of our time, a dear little seaside place with beautiful woods, just then in their full glory of autumnal colouring. It was within easy reach of Copenhagen and we went in almost every day, for one reason or another, and grew very fond of the beautiful old city.

The time came for us to say good-bye. I was very sorry indeed to leave dear little Denmark where we had had such a warm welcome. Denmark is, of course, officially, absolutely neutral, but she cannot forget the ties of blood and friendship that bind the two island countries together. They are indeed a splendid people to be kin to, tall and fair and strong, as becomes an ancient race of sea-kings. I only hope that it may be my good fortune, some day, to be able to repay in some small measure all the wealth of kindness so freely poured out for us.

On Saturday, October 24, at 7 P.M. we started for Lapland! Many of our very kind friends came down to the station to give us a good send-off and with last presents of flowers, fruit, chocolates and papers. We crossed first to Malmö on the ferry, which took about an hour and a half. It was very calm and clear, and we watched the little twinkling lights of Denmark gradually disappear and the lights of Sweden gradually

A Peaceful Interlude

emerge in exchange. At Malmö there was a customs examination which was not very severe, as our things were all marked with a huge Red Cross, and then we got into a funny little horse tram that conveyed us to the station.

When morning broke we were speeding along towards Stockholm. The country was very different from Denmark, much wilder, with rocks and trees and sand and an occasional glimpse of lake. At that time Sweden was supposed to bear little good-will towards England, and certainly our reception in that land was distinctly a chilly one. We drove on arrival to a hotel which had been recommended to us and asked the concierge if there were rooms. He said there were, so we had our luggage taken down and dismissed the cab. The concierge then looked at us suspiciously, and said, "You are English?" "Yes, we are English." He then went and confabbed for some minutes with the manageress, and returned. "There are people still in the rooms, they will not be ready for twenty minutes." "Then we will have breakfast now and go to our rooms after." Another long conversation with the manageress, and then he returned again. "There are no rooms." "But you said there were rooms." "There are no rooms." Evidently there were none for English travellers anyway, so we went to another hotel opposite the station, where they were civil, but no more. We had to stay in Stockholm twenty-four hours and simply hated it. I had heard much of this "Venice of the North," but the physical atmosphere was as chilly and unfriendly as the mental one.

The recollection stamped on my memory is of a grey, cheerless town where it rained hard almost the whole time, and a bitter wind blowing over the quays which moaned and sobbed like a lost banshee.

I was asked to luncheon at the British Legation, and this proved a very fortunate occurrence for us all, as the minister was so kind as to go to great trouble in getting us a special permit from the Swedish Foreign Office to sleep at Boden. Boden is a fortified frontier town and no foreigners are, as a rule, allowed to stay the night there, but have to go on to Lulea, and return to Boden the next morning. We started off on the next

A Peaceful Interlude

lap of our northern journey that evening, and again through the minister's kind intervention were lucky in getting a carriage to ourselves in a very full train, and arrived twenty-four hours later at Boden.

It was extraordinarily interesting to sleep in that little shanty at Boden, partly, no doubt, because it was not ordinarily allowed. The forbidden has always charms. It was the most glorious starlight night I have ever seen, but bitterly cold, with the thermometer ten degrees below zero, and everything sparkling with hoar frost. It was here we nearly lost a bishop. A rather pompous Anglican bishop had been travelling in the same train from Stockholm, and hearing that we insignificant females had been permitted to sleep at Boden, he did not see why he should not do the same and save himself the tiresome journey to Lulea and back. So in spite of all remonstrances he insisted on alighting at Boden, and with the whole force of his ecclesiastical authority announced his intention of staying there. However, it was not allowed after all, and he missed the train, and while we were comfortably having our supper in the little inn, we saw the poor bishop and his chaplain being driven off to Lulea. They turned up again next morning, but so late that we were afraid they had got lost on the way the night before.

All the next morning we went through the same kind of country, past innumerable frozen lakelets, and copses of stubby pines and silver birches, till we arrived at Karungi where the railway ends. We made friends with a most delightful man, who was so good in helping us all the way through that we christened him St. Raphael, the patron saint of travellers. He was a fur trader from Finland, and had immense stores of information about the land and the queer beasts that live in it. He was a sociable soul, but lived in such out-of-the-way places that he seldom saw anyone to talk to except the peasants, and it was a great treat, he said, to meet some of his fellow-countrymen, and his satisfaction knew no bounds when he heard that one of us hailed from Lancashire, near his old home.

From Karungi we had to drive to Haparanda. Our carriage was already booked by telegram, but a very irate gentleman from Port Said got into it with his family

A Peaceful Interlude

and declined to get out, using such dreadful language that I wondered the snow did not begin to sizzle. We did not want to have a scene there, so when "St. Raphael" said if we would wait till the evening he would take us over by starlight, we graciously let the dusky gentleman with the bad temper keep our carriage.

We went in the meantime to the little wooden inn and ate largely of strange dishes, dried reindeer flesh, smoked strips of salmon, lax, I think it is called, served with a curious sweet sauce, and drank many glasses of tea. At 9 P.M. behold an open motor-car arrived to take us the thirty miles' drive to Haparanda. It seemed absolutely absurd to see a motor-car up there on the edge of the Arctic Circle, where there was not even a proper road. There were several reindeer sleighs about, and I felt that one of those would have been much more in keeping. The drivers look most attractive, they wear very gay reindeer leggings, big sheep-skin coats and wild-looking wolf-skin caps.

The frozen track was so uneven that we rocked from side to side, and were thrown violently about in the car, like little kernels in a very large nut. But it was a wonderful night all the same, the air was thin and intoxicating like champagne, and the stars up in these northern latitudes more dazzlingly brilliant than anything I have seen before. We had to get out at Haparanda and walk over the long bridge which led to Torneo, where the Finnish Custom House was, and where our luggage and passports had to be examined.

We arrived there very cheerful and well pleased with ourselves, to find all our old travelling companions waiting till the Custom House was open ; the bishop and his party ; the bad-tempered man and his family ; a Russian and a Chinese student who were travelling together, and some others. They had been waiting in the cold for hours, and had not had their papers or luggage examined yet, so we had had the best of it after all.

And we scored yet once more, for "St. Raphael," who spoke fluent Finnish, at once secured the only cart to take our things over the ferry to the railway station about half a mile away.

It was borne in upon me during this journey what an immense country Russia

A Peaceful Interlude

is. From Torneo to Petrograd does not look far on the map, but we left Torneo on Wednesday night, and did not arrive in Petrograd till 12.30 A.M. on Saturday, about fifty-two hours' hard travelling to cover this little track—a narrow thread, almost lost the immensity of this great Empire.

Petrograd is not one of those cities whose charms steal upon you unawares. It is immense, insistent, arresting, almost thrusting itself on your imagination. It is a city for giants to dwell in, everything is on such an enormous scale, dealt out in such careless profusion. The river, first of all, is immense; the palaces grandiose, the very blocks of which they are fashioned seem to have been hewn by Titans. The names are full of romance and mystery. The fortress of St. Peter and St. Paul, for instance, how it brings back a certain red and gold book of one's youth, full of innocent prisoners in clanking chains confined in fetid underground dungeons. It seemed incredible to really behold its slender, golden minarets on the other side of the Neva. But this was no time for sight-seeing, we were all very anxious to get to work at once. So my first excursion in Petrograd was to the Central Bureau of the Red Cross.

The director of the Red Cross received me most kindly and promised that we should have work very soon. He suggested that in the meantime we should go and stay in a Russian Community of Sisters, who had a hospital in Petrograd. I was very glad to accept this offer for us all, for we must assimilate Russian methods and ways of thought as soon as possible, if we were to be of real use to them. Still I very much hoped that we should not be kept in Petrograd very long, as we wanted, if possible, to get nearer the front. I told the director that we had been inoculated against cholera and typhoid, and would be quite pleased to be sent to the infectious hospitals if that would be more help, as there are always plenty of people to nurse the wounded, but comparatively few who for one reason or another are able to devote themselves to this other very necessary work.

We betook ourselves without delay to the Community of Russian Sisters, and were installed in dear little cell-like rooms at the top of the house devoted to the Sisters. The

A Peaceful Interlude

other side of the house is a beautiful little hospital with several wards set apart for wounded soldiers. There are a great many similar communities in Russia—all nursing orders. They are called Sisters of Mercy, but are not nuns in any sense, as they take no vows and are free to leave whenever they like. The course of training varies from two to three years and is very complete, comprising courses in dispensing and other useful subjects. The pity of it is that there are comparatively few of these trained Sisters at the front; the vast majority of those working there have only been through a special "War Course" of two months' training, and are apt to think that bandaging is the beginning and the end of the art of nursing.

The Russian Sisters were most interested in our adventures, and most kind and nice to us in every way, but assured us that we should not be allowed anywhere near the front, as only Russian Sisters were allowed there. They were very surprised when the order came a few days after our arrival, that we were to get ready to go to Warsaw at once. That was certainly not quite at the front at that moment, as just then Russia was in the flush of victory, following the retreating Germans back from Warsaw to the German frontier. But it was a good long step on the way.

One errand still remained to be done. I had not posted the letter given me by the English lady at the Brussels station to her husband in Petrograd, wishing to have the pleasure of delivering it myself after carrying it at such risks all through Germany. Directly I arrived I made inquiries for this Englishman, picturing his joy at getting the long-deferred news of his wife. Almost the first person I asked knew him quite well, but imagine what a blow it was to hear that he had a Russian wife in Petrograd! I vowed never again to carry any more letters to sorrowing husbands.

Before we went I received a very kind message that the Empress Marie Federovna would like to see us before our departure. Prince Gustav of Denmark had been most kind in writing to his aunt, the Empress, about us, and had also been good enough to give me a letter of introduction to her which I sent through the British Embassy.

A day was appointed to go to the Gatchina

A Peaceful Interlude

Palace to be presented to her Majesty. The palace is a little way out of Petrograd and stands in a beautiful park between the Black and the White Lake.

We were greeted by General K——, one of the Empress's bodyguard, and waited for a few minutes in the throne room downstairs, chatting to him. Soon we were summoned upstairs, a door was thrown open by an enormous negro in scarlet livery, and we were ushered into the Empress's private boudoir. The Empress was there, and was absolutely charming to us, making us sit down beside her and talking to us in fluent English. She was so interested in hearing all we could tell her of Belgium, and we stayed about half an hour talking to her. Then the Empress rose and held out her hand, and said, "Thank you very much for coming to help us in Russia. I shall always be interested in hearing about you. May God bless you in your work," and we were dismissed.

I would not have missed that for anything, it seemed such a nice start to our work in Russia.

Every spare moment till our work began

had to be devoted to learning Russian. It is a brain-splitting language. Before I went to Russia I was told that two words would carry me through the Empire: "Nichevo" meaning "never mind," and "Seechas" which means "immediately" or "to-morrow" or "next week." But we had to study every moment to learn as much Russian as possible, as of course the soldiers could not understand any other language. French is understood everywhere in society, but in the shops no other tongue than Russian is any use. German is understood pretty widely— but it is absolutely forbidden now to be spoken under penalty of a 3000 rouble fine. In all the hotels there is a big notice put up in Russian, French, and English in the public rooms "It is forbidden to speak German," and just at first it added rather to the complications of life not to be able to use it.

VII

OUR WORK IN WARSAW

IN two or three days' time after our visit to the Empress we were off to Warsaw and reported ourselves to Monsieur Goochkoff, the head of the Red Cross Society there.

We received our marching orders at once. We were not to be together at first, as they thought we should learn Russian more quickly if we were separated, so two of us were to go to one hospital in Warsaw, two to another. My fate was a large Red Cross hospital close to the station, worked by a Community of Russian Sisters. I must say I had some anxious moments as I drove with Sister G. to the hospital that afternoon. I wondered if Monsieur Goochkoff had said we were coming, and thought if two Russian Sisters suddenly turned up without notice at an English hospital how very much surprised they would be. Then I hoped they were very busy, as perhaps then they would welcome our help. But again, I meditated, if they were really busy, we with our stumbling Russian phrases might be only in the way. It was all very well in Denmark to think one would come and help Russia—but supposing they did not want us after all?

By the time I got so far we had arrived at the hospital, the old familiar hospital smell of disinfectants met my nostrils, and I felt at home at once. I found that I had been tormenting myself in vain, for they were expecting us and apparently were not at all displeased at our arrival. The Sister Superior had worked with English people in the Russo-Japanese War and spoke English almost perfectly, and several of the other Sisters spoke French or German. She was very worried as to where we should sleep, as they were dreadfully overcrowded themselves; even she had shared her small room with another Sister. However, she finally found us a corner in a room which already held six Sisters. Eight of us in a small room with only one window! The Sisters sleeping there took our advent like angels, said there was plenty of room, and moved

Our Work in Warsaw

their beds closer together so that we might have more space. Again I wondered whether if it were England we should be quite so amiable under like circumstances. I hope so.

I began to unpack, but there was nowhere to put anything; there was no furniture in the room whatsoever except our straw beds, a table, and a large tin basin behind a curtain in which we all washed—and, of course, the ikon or holy picture which hangs in every Russian room. We all kept our belongings under our beds—not a very hygienic proceeding, but *à la guerre comme à la guerre.* The patients were very overcrowded too, every corridor was lined with beds, and the sanitars, or orderlies, slept on straw mattresses in the hall. The hospital had been a large college and was originally arranged to hold five hundred patients, but after the last big battle at Soldau every hospital in Warsaw was crammed with wounded, and more than nine hundred patients had been sent in here and had to be squeezed into every available corner.

My work was in the dressing-room, which meant dressing wounds all day and sometimes well into the night, and whatever time we finished there were all the dressings for the next day to be cut and prepared before we could go to bed. The first week was one long nightmare with the awful struggle for the Russian names of dressings and instruments and with their different methods of working, but after that I settled down very happily.

Sister G. was in the operating-room on the next floor, and she, too, found that first week a great strain. The other two Sisters who had come out with us and had been sent to another hospital apparently found the same, for they returned to England after the first five days, much to my disappointment, as I had hoped that our little unit of four might have got a small job of our own later, when we could speak Russian better and had learnt their ways and customs.

After the first few days we began to be very busy. In England we should consider that hospital very badly staffed, as there were only twenty Sisters to sometimes nearly a thousand patients, all very serious cases moreover, as we were not supposed to take in the lightly wounded at all in this hospital. The sanitars, or orderlies, do all

Our Work in Warsaw

that probationers in an English hospital would do for the patients, and all the heavy lifting and carrying, so that the work is not very hard though very continuous. There was no night staff. We all took it in turns to stay up at night three at a time, so that our turn came about once a week. That meant being on duty all day, all night, and all the next day, except for a brief rest and a walk in the afternoon. Most of the Sisters took no exercise beyond one weekly walk, but we two English people longed for fresh air, and went out whenever possible even if it was only for ten minutes. English views on ventilation are not at all accepted in Russia. It is a great concession to open the windows of the ward for ten minutes twice a day to air it, and the Sisters were genuinely frightened for the safety of the patients when I opened the windows of a hot, stuffy ward one night. "It is *never* done," they reiterated, "before daylight."

The Sister Superior was the mainspring of the hospital. She really was a wonderful person, small and insignificant to look at, except for her eyes, which looked you through and through and weighed you in the balance; absolutely true and straight, with a heart of gold, and the very calmest person in all the world. I remember her, late one evening, when everybody was rather agitated at a message which had come to say that 400 patients were on their way to the hospital, and room could only be made for 200 at the most. "Never mind," she said, not in the least perturbed, "they must be made as comfortable as possible on stretchers for the night, and to-morrow we must get some of the others moved away." And the Sisters took their cue from her, and those 400 patients were all taken in and looked after with less fuss than the arrival of forty unexpected patients in most hospitals.

All night long that procession of shattered men brought in on stretchers never ceased. The kitchen Sister stayed up all night so that each man should have some hot soup on arrival, and all the other Sisters were at their posts. Each man was undressed on the stretcher (often so badly wounded that all his clothing had to be cut off him) and hastily examined by the doctor. He was then dressed in a clean cotton shirt and trousers and lifted into bed, either to enjoy a bowl of hot soup, or, if the case was urgent, to be taken off in his turn to the operating-room. And though she was no longer young and not at all strong, there was dear Sister Superior herself all night, taking round the big bowls of soup or sitting beside the dying patients to cheer and comfort their last hours. How the men loved her.

It was she who gave the whole tone to the hospital—there the patients and their welfare were the first consideration and nothing else mattered in comparison. The hospital was not "smart" or "up to date," the wards were not even tidy, the staff was inadequate, overworked, and villainously housed, the resources very scanty, but for sheer selflessness and utter devotion to their work the staff of that hospital from top to bottom could not have been surpassed. I never heard a grumble or a complaint all the time I was there either from a doctor, a Sister, or an orderly, and I never saw in this hospital a dressing slurred over, omitted, or done without the usual precautions however tired or overworked everybody might be.

Field Hospital & Flying Column

Of course the art of nursing as practised in England does not exist in Russia—even the trained Sisters do things every hour that would horrify us in England. One example of this is their custom of giving strong narcotic or stimulating drugs indiscriminately, such as morphine, codeine, camphor, or ether without doctors' orders. When untrained Sisters and inexperienced dressers do this (which constantly happens) the results are sometimes very deplorable. I have myself seen a dresser give a strong hypodermic stimulant to a man with a very serious hæmorrhage. The bleeding vessel was deep down and very difficult to find, and the hæmorrhage became so severe after the stimulant that for a long time his life was despaired of from extreme exhaustion due to loss of blood. I have also heard a Sister with no training except the two months' war course say she had given a certain man *ten* injections of camphor within an hour because he was so collapsed, but she had not seen fit to tell the doctor she had done this, nor had she let him know his patient was so much worse until he was at the point of death. Neither of these

Our Work in Warsaw

particular incidents could have happened in the Red Cross hospital at Warsaw as the Sisters there were properly trained; but even there they gave drugs at their own sweet will without consulting anyone—particularly in the night.

We were so busy at the hospital that we did not see much of Warsaw. To the casual observer it looks a busy, modern, rather gay capital, but almost every inch of the city is interesting historically, and nearly all the pages of that history are red with blood. War, revolutions, and riots seem to have been almost its normal condition, and the great broad Vistula that flows sluggishly through it has been many a time before stained crimson with the blood of its citizens. But this time the war is being fought under different conditions. Russians and Poles are for the first time working together with a common aim in view. If the only outcome of this war was the better mutual understanding of these two great nations, it would not have been fought entirely in vain.

When we first arrived the Russians had beaten the Germans back to the frontier, and every one was elated with the great victory. Now at the end of October things did not look quite so happy. The people who knew looked anxious and harassed. The newspapers, as usual, told nothing at all, but the news which always filters in somehow from mouth to mouth was not good. Terrific fighting was going on outside Lodz, it was said, and enormous German reinforcements were being poured in. Warsaw was full to overflowing with troops going through to reinforce on the Russian side. A splendid set of men they looked, sturdy, broad-chested, and hardy—not in the least smart, but practical and efficient in their warm brown overcoats and big top boots.

There are two things one notices at once about the Russian soldier. One is his absolute disregard of appearances. If he is cold he will tie a red comforter round his head without minding in the least whether he is in the most fashionable street in Warsaw or in camp at the front. The other noticeable characteristic is the friendly terms he is on with his officers. The Prussian soldiers rarely seem to like their officers, and it is not to be wondered at, as they treat their men in a very harsh, overbearing way. On duty the Russian discipline is strict, but off duty an officer may be heard addressing one of his men as " little pigeon " or " comrade " and other terms of endearment, and the soldier, on the other hand, will call his officer " little father " or " little brother." I remember one most touching scene when a soldier servant accompanied his wounded officer to hospital. The officer was quite a young, delicate-looking boy, who had been shot through the chest. His servant was a huge, rough Cossack, who would hardly let any of us touch his master if he could help it, and stayed by his bed night and day till the end, when, his great frame heaving with sobs and tears streaming down the seamed and rugged face, he threw himself over the officer's body and implored God to let him die too.

The hospital began to grow empty and the work slackened down, as every possible patient was sent away to Moscow or Petrograd to make room for the rush of wounded that must be coming from the Lodz direction. But no patients arrived, and we heard that the railway communications had been cut. But this proved to be untrue.

One Sunday afternoon Sister G. and I,

being free, betook ourselves to tea at the Hotel d'Europe—that well-named hostelry which has probably seen more history made from its windows than any other hotel in Europe. We favoured it always on Sunday when we could, for not only was a particularly nice tea to be had, but one could also read there a not *too* old French newspaper. I think just at first we felt almost as cut off from news of what was happening on the English side as we did in Belgium. No English or French papers could be bought and the Polish and Russian papers were as sealed books to us, and when I did succeed in getting some long-suffering person to translate them to me, the news was naturally chiefly of the doings of the Russian side. Later on I had English papers sent out to me which kept me in touch with the western front, and also by that time, too, I could make out the substance of the Russian papers; but just at first it was very trying not to know what was going on. We had had tea and had read of an Anglo-French success near Ypres and returned rested and cheered to the hospital to find Sister Superior asking for us. She

Our Work in Warsaw

had had a message from the Red Cross Office that we were to go to Lodz next day, and were to go at once to the Hotel Bristol to meet Prince V., who would give us full particulars.

We went off at once to the Bristol and saw Prince V., but did not get any particulars—that was not the Prince's way. He was sitting reading in the lounge when we arrived, a very tall, lean, handsome man with kind brown eyes and a nose hooked like an eagle's. He greeted us very kindly and said he would take us to Lodz next day in one of the Red Cross automobiles, and that we must be ready at 10 A.M. I think we earned his everlasting gratitude by asking no questions as to where and how we were going to work, but simply said we would be ready at that time and returned to hospital to pack, fully realizing what lucky people we were to be going right into the thick of things, and only hoping that we should rise to the occasion and do the utmost that was expected of us.

We were now officially transferred from the hospital to the Flying Column, of which Prince V. was the head. A flying column

Field Hospital & Flying Column

works directly under the head of the Red Cross, and is supposed to go anywhere and do anything at any hour of the day or night. Our Column consisted of five automobiles that conveyed us and all our equipment to the place where we were to work, and then were engaged in fetching in wounded, and taking them on to the field hospital or ambulance train. The staff consisted of Prince and Princess V., we two English Sisters, with generally, but not always, some Russian ones in addition, an English surgeon, Colonel S., some Russian dressers and students, and some sanitars, or orderlies. The luggage was a dreadful problem, and the Prince always groaned at the amount we would take with us, but we could not reduce it, as we had to carry big cases of cotton-wool, bandages and dressings, anæsthetics, field sterilizer, operating-theatre equipment, and a certain amount of stores—such as soap, candles, benzine and tinned food—as the column would have been quite useless if it had not been to a large extent self-supporting. Our Column was attached to the Second Army, which operated on the eastern front of

Our Work in Warsaw

Warsaw. The Russian front changes so much more rapidly than the Anglo-French front, where progress is reckoned in metres, that these mobile columns are a great feature of ambulance work here. Our front changed many miles in a week sometimes, so that units that can move anywhere at an hour's notice are very useful. The big base hospitals cannot quite fulfil the same need on such a rapidly changing front.

VIII

THE BOMBARDMENT OF LODZ

It took us a long time to get to Lodz, though it is not much more than 200 kilometres away. Russian roads are villainously bad anyhow, and the Germans, though their retreat had been hasty, had had time to destroy the roads and bridges as they went. Another thing that delayed us were the enormous reinforcements of troops going up from Warsaw to the front. It was very interesting to watch the different groups as we passed, first a Cossack regiment going up, then an immense convoy followed with about 200 wagons of forage. Just ahead of that we passed the remounts—sturdy, shaggy Siberian ponies. They are the most delightful creatures in the world, as tame as a dog, and not much bigger, and many of them of a most unusual and beautiful shade of golden cream. They have been brought from

MAP OF THE POLISH FRONT

The Bombardment of Lodz

Siberia by the thousand, and most of the little things had never seen a motor-car before, and pranced and kicked and jumped, and went through all kinds of circus tricks as we passed.

As we grew nearer to Lodz it was sad to see a good many dead horses lying by the roadside, mostly killed by shell-fire. The shells had made great holes in the road too, and the last part of our journey was like a ride on a switchback railway. It began to get dark as we came to Breeziny, where a large number of Russian batteries were stationed. It looked very jolly there, these large camps of men and horses having their supper by the light of a camp-fire, with only the distant rumble of the guns to remind them that they were at war. Two hours later we jolted into the streets of Lodz.

Lodz is a large cotton manufacturing town—sometimes called the Manchester of Poland—but now of course all the factories were closed, and many destroyed by shell. I should not think it was a very festive place at the best of times; it looked squalid and grimy, and the large bulk of its population was made up of the most abject Jews I have ever seen.

We had to make a long detour and get into the town by an unfrequented country road, as Lodz was being heavily bombarded by the German guns. We were put down at a large building which we were told was the military hospital. Princess V., Colonel S., and a Russian student were working hard in the operating-room, and we hastily put on clean overalls and joined them. They all looked absolutely worn out, and the doctor dropped asleep between each case; but fresh wounded were being brought in every minute and there was no one else to help. Lodz was one big hospital. We heard that there were more than 18,000 wounded there, and I can well believe it. Every building of any size had been turned into a hospital, and almost all the supplies of every kind had given out.

The building we were in had been a day-school, and the top floor was made up of large airy schoolrooms that were quite suitable for wards. But the shelling recommenced so violently that the wounded all had to be moved down to the ground floor and into the cellars. The place was an absolute inferno. I could never have imagined anything worse. It was fearfully cold, and the hospital was not heated at all, for there was no wood or coal in Lodz, and for the same reason the gas-jets gave out only the faintest glimmer of light. There was no clean linen, and the poor fellows were lying there still in their verminous, blood-soaked shirts, shivering with cold, as we had only one small blanket each for them. They were lucky if they had a bed at all, for many were lying with only a little straw between them and the cold stone floor. There were no basins or towels or anything to wash up with, and no spittoons, so the men were spitting all over the already filthy floor. In the largest ward where there were seventy or eighty men lying, there was a lavatory adjoining which had got blocked up, and a thin stream of dirty water trickled under the door and meandered in little rivulets all over the room. The smell was awful, as some of the men had been there already several days without having had their dressings done.

This was the state in which the hospital had

been handed over to us. It was a military hospital whose staff had had orders to leave at four o'clock that morning, and they handed the whole hospital with its 270 patients over to us just as it was; and we could do very little towards making it more comfortable for them. The stench of the whole place was horrible, but it was too cold to do more than open the window for a minute or two every now and then. It was no one's fault that things were in such a horrible condition —it was just the force of circumstances and the fortune of war that the place had been taxed far beyond its possible capacities.

All night long the most terribly wounded men were being brought in from the field, some were already dead when they arrived, others had only a few minutes to live; all the rest were very cold and wet and exhausted, and we had *nothing* to make them comfortable. What a blessing hot-water bottles would have been—but after all there would have been no hot water to fill them if we had had them. But the wounded *had* to be brought in for shelter somewhere, and at least we had a roof over their heads, and hot tea to give them.

The Bombardment of Lodz

At 5 A.M. there came a lull. The tragic procession ceased for a while, and we went to lie down. At seven o'clock we were called again—another batch of wounded was being brought in.

The shelling had begun again, and was terrific; crash, crash, over our heads the whole time. A clock-tower close to the hospital was demolished and windows broken everywhere. The shells were bursting everywhere in the street, and civilians were being brought in to us severely wounded. A little child was carried in with half its head blown open, and then an old Jewish woman with both legs blown off, and a terrible wound in her chest, who only lived an hour or two. Apparently she suffered no pain, but was most dreadfully agitated, poor old dear, at having lost her wig in the transit. They began bringing in so many that we had to stop civilians being brought in at all, as it was more than we could do to cope with the wounded soldiers that were being brought in all the time.

At midday we went to a hotel for a meal. There was very, very little food left in Lodz, but they brought what they could. Coming back to the hospital we tried everywhere to get some bread, but there was none to be had anywhere—all the provision shops were quite empty, and the inhabitants looked miserable and starved, the Jewish population particularly so, though they were probably not among the poorest.

On our way back a shell burst quite close to us in the street, but no one was hurt. These shells make a most horrible scream before bursting, like an animal in pain. Ordinarily I am the most dreadful coward in the world about loud noises—I even hate a sham thunderstorm in a theatre—but here somehow the shells were so part of the whole thing that one did not realize that all this was happening to *us*, one felt rather like a disinterested spectator at a far-off dream. It was probably partly due to want of sleep; one's hands did the work, but one's mind was mercifully numbed. Mercifully, for it was more like hell than anything I can imagine. The never-ending processions of groaning men being brought in on those horrible blood-soaked stretchers, suffering unimagined tortures, the filth, the cold, the stench, the hunger, the vermin, and the

The Bombardment of Lodz

squalor of it all, added to one's utter helplessness to do more than very little to relieve their misery, was almost enough to make even Satan weep.

On the third day after our arrival a young Russian doctor and some Russian sisters arrived to relieve us for a few hours, and we most thankfully went to bed—at least it was not a bed in the ordinary sense, but a wire bedstead on which we lay down in all our clothes; but we were very comfortable all the same.

When we woke up we were told that the military authorities had given orders for the patients to be evacuated, and that Red Cross carts were coming all night to take them away to the station, where some ambulance trains awaited them. So we worked hard all night to get the dressings done before the men were sent away, and as we finished each case, he was carried down to the hall to await his turn to go; but it was very difficult as all the time they were bringing in fresh cases as fast as they were taking the others away, and alas! many had to go off without having had their dressings done at all. The next afternoon we were still taking in, when we got another order that all the fresh patients were to be evacuated and the hospital closed, as the Russians had decided to retire from Lodz. Again we worked all night, and by ten the next morning we had got all the patients away. The sanitars collected all the bedding in the yard to be burnt, the bedsteads were piled high on one another, and we opened all the windows wide to let the clean cold wind blow over everything.

We had all our own dressings and equipment to pack, and were all just about at our last gasp from want of food and sleep, when a very kind Polish lady came and carried princess, we two Sisters, and Colonel S. off to her house, where she had prepared bedrooms for us. I never looked forward to anything so much in my life as I did to my bed that night. Our hostess simply heaped benefits on us by preparing us each a hot bath in turn. We had not washed or had our clothes off since we came to Lodz, and were covered with vermin which had come to us from the patients; men and officers alike suffer terribly from this plague of insects, which really do make one's life a

The Bombardment of Lodz

burden. There are three varieties commonly met with: ordinary fleas that no one minds in the least; white insects that are the commonest and live in the folds of one's clothes, whose young are most difficult to find, and who grow middle-aged and very hungry in a single night; and, lastly, the red insects with a good many legs, which are much less numerous but much more ravenous than the other kinds.

After the bath and the hunt, we sat down to a delicious supper, and were looking forward to a still more delicious night in bed, when suddenly Prince V. arrived and said we must leave at once. We guessed instantly that the Germans must be very near, but that he did not wish us to ask questions, as it seemed very mean to go off ourselves and leave our kind hosts without a word of explanation, though of course we could only obey orders. So we left our unfinished supper and quickly collected our belongings and took them to the hotel where our Red Cross car should have been waiting for us. But the Red Cross authorities had sent off our car with some wounded, which of course was just as it should be, and we were promised another "seechas," which literally translated signifies "immediately," but in Russia means to-day or to-morrow or not at all.

"Let us come into the hotel and get a meal while we wait," suggested the Prince, mindful of our uneaten supper, and we followed him to the restaurant—still mourning those beautiful beds we had left behind us, and so tired we didn't much care whether the Germans came or not. Nothing can express utter desolation much more nakedly than a Grand Hotel that has been through a week or two's bombardment. Here indeed were the mighty fallen. A large hole was ripped out of the wall of the big restaurant, close to the alcove where the band used to play while the smart people dined. An elaborate wine-list still graced each little table, but coffee made from rye bread crusts mixed with a little chicory was the only drink that a few white-faced waiters who crept about the room like shadows could apologetically offer us. We sat there till nearly 3 A.M., and Colonel S., utterly worn out, was fast asleep with his head on the little table, and there was no sign of any car, or of

The Bombardment of Lodz

any Germans, so we went to lie down till morning.

In the morning things began to look cheerful. The Germans had still not arrived, our own car turned up, and best of all the Prince heard officially that every wounded man who was at all transportable had now been successfully got out of Lodz. It was a gigantic task, this evacuation of over 18,000 wounded in four days, and it is a great feather in the Russian cap to have achieved it so successfully.

It was a most lovely day with a soft blue sky, and all the world bathed in winter sunshine. Shelling had ceased during the night, but began again with terrific force in the morning, and we started off under a perfect hail of shells. There were four German aeroplanes hovering just above us, throwing down bombs at short intervals. The shells aimed at them looked so innocent, like little white puff-balls bursting up in the blue sky. We hoped they would be brought down, but they were too high for that. The bombs were only a little diversion of theirs by the way—they were really trying to locate the Russian battery, as they were evidently making signals to their own headquarters. Danger always adds a spice to every entertainment, and as the wounded were all out and we had nobody but ourselves to think about, we could enjoy our thrilling departure from Lodz under heavy fire to the uttermost. And I must say I have rarely enjoyed anything more. It was simply glorious spinning along in that car, and we got out safely without anyone being hurt.

We passed through Breeziny, where the tail-end of a battle was going on, and the Prince stopped the car for a few minutes so that we could see the men in the trenches. On our way we passed crowds of terrified refugees hurrying along the road with their few possessions on their backs or in their arms; it reminded me of those sad processions of flying peasants in Belgium, but I think these were mostly much poorer, and had not so much to lose. Just as the sun was setting we stopped for a rest at a place the Prince knew of, half inn, half farm-house. We looked back, and the sky was bloody and lurid over the western plain where Lodz lay. To us it seemed like an ill omen for the unhappy town, but it may be that the Germans

The Bombardment of Lodz

took those flaming clouds to mean that even the heavens themselves were illuminated to signal their victory.

Some bread and some pale golden Hungarian Tokay were produced by our host for our refreshment. The latter was delicious, but it must have been much more potent than it looked, for though I only had one small glass of it, I collapsed altogether afterwards, and lay on the floor of the car, and could not move till the lights of Warsaw were in sight. In a few minutes more we arrived at the Hotel Bristol, and then the Flying Column went to bed at last.

IX

MORE DOINGS OF THE FLYING COLUMN

THE Grand Duchess Cyril happened to be staying at the Hotel Bristol too. Like most of the other members of the Russian Royal Family, since the beginning of the war she has been devoting her whole time to helping wounded soldiers, and is the centre of a whole network of activities. She has a large hospital in Warsaw for men and officers, a very efficient ambulance train that can hold 800 wounded, and one of the best surgeons in Petrograd working on it, and a provision train which sets up feeding-stations for the troops and for refugees in places where food is very scarce, which last is an indescribable boon to all who benefit by it. The Grand Duchess's hospital in Warsaw, like every other just at this time, was crammed to overflowing with wounded from Lodz, and the staff

More Doings of the Flying Column

was inadequate to meet this unexpected need.

The Grand Duchess met Princess V. in the lounge just as we arrived from Lodz, and begged that our Column might go and help for a time at her hospital. Accordingly, the next day, the consent of the Red Cross Office having been obtained, we went off to the Grand Duchess's hospital for a time to supplement and relieve their staff. They met us with open arms, as they were all very tired and very thankful for our help. They only had room for fifty patients and had had about 150 brought in. Fortunately the Grand Duchess's ambulance train had just come back to Warsaw, so the most convalescent of the old cases were taken off to Petrograd, but even then we were working in the operating-theatre till twelve or one every night. They hoped we had come for two or three weeks and were very disgusted when, in five days' time, the order came for us to go off to Skiernevice with the automobiles. The hospital staff gave us such a nice send-off, and openly wished that they belonged to a flying column too. I must say it was very interesting these

Field Hospital & Flying Column

startings off into the unknown, with our little fleet of automobiles containing ourselves and our equipment. We made a very flourishing start out of Warsaw, but very soon plunged into an appalling mess of mud. One could really write an epic poem on Russian roads. At the best of times they are awful; on this particular occasion they were full of large holes made by shells and covered with thick swampy mud that had been snow the week before. It delayed us so much that we did not get to Skiernevice till late that night.

Skiernevice is a small town, important chiefly as a railway junction, as two lines branch off here towards Germany and Austria north-west and south-west. The Tsar has a shooting - box here in the midst of beautiful woods, and two rooms had been set apart in this house for our Column.

We arrived late in the evening, secretly hoping that we should get a night in bed, and were rather rejoiced at finding that there were no wounded there at all at present, though a large contingent was expected later. So we camped in the two

More Doings of the Flying Column

rooms allotted to us: Princess, Sister G., and myself in one, and all the men of the party in the other. No wounded arrived for two or three days, and we thoroughly enjoyed the rest and, above all, the beautiful woods. How delicious the pines smelt after that horrible Lodz. Twice a day we used to go down the railway line, where there was a restaurant car for the officers; it seemed odd to be eating our meals in the Berlin-Warsaw International Restaurant Car. There was always something interesting going on at the station. One day a regiment from Warsaw had just been detrained there when a German Taube came sailing over the station throwing down grenades. Every man immediately began to fire up in the air, and we ran much more risk of being killed by a Russian bullet than by the German Taube. It was like being in the middle of a battle, and I much regretted I had not my camera with me. Another day all the débris of a battlefield had been picked up and was lying in piles in the station waiting to be sent off to Warsaw. There were truck-loads of stuff; German and Russian overcoats, boots, rifles, water-bottles, caps, swords, and helmets and all sorts of miscellaneous kit.

We often saw gangs of prisoners, mostly Austrian, but some German, and they always seemed well treated by the Russians. The Austrian prisoners nearly always looked very miserable, cold, hungry, and worn out. Once we saw a spy being put into the train to go to Warsaw, I suppose to be shot—an old Jewish man with white hair in a long, black gaberdine, strips of coloured paper still in his hand with which he had been caught signalling to the Germans. *How* angry the soldiers were with him—one gave him a great punch in the back, another kicked him up into the train, and a soldier on the platform who saw what was happening ran as fast as he could and was just in time to give him a parting hit on the shoulder. The old man did not cry out or attempt to retaliate, but his face was ashy-white with terror, and one of his hands was dripping with blood. It was a very horrible sight and haunted me all the rest of the day. It was quite right that he should be shot as a spy, but the unnecessary cruelty first sickened me.

More Doings of the Flying Column

There were masses of troops constantly going up to the positions from Skiernevice, and as there was a short cut through the park, which they generally used, we could see all that was going on from our rooms. On Sunday it was evident that another big battle was pending. Several batteries went up through our woods, each gun-carriage almost up to its axles in mud, dragged by eight strong horses. They were followed by a regiment of Cossacks, looking very fierce in their great black fur head-dresses, huge sheep-skin coats, and long spears. There was one small Cossack boy who was riding out with his father to the front and who could not have been more than eleven or twelve years old. There are quite a number of young boys at the front who make themselves very useful in taking messages, carrying ammunition, and so on. We had one little boy of thirteen in the hospital at Warsaw, who was badly wounded while carrying a message to the colonel, and he was afterwards awarded the St. George's Cross.

There were enormous numbers of other troops too: Siberians, Tartars, Asiatic

Field Hospital & Flying Column

Russians from Turkestan, Caucasians in their beautiful black-and-silver uniforms, Little Russians from the south, and great fair-haired giants from the north.

The little Catholic Church in the village was full to overflowing at the early Mass that Sunday morning with men in full marching kit on their way out to the trenches. A very large number of them made their Confession and received the Blessed Sacrament before starting out, and for many, many of these it was their Viaticum, for the great battle began that afternoon, and few of the gallant fellows we saw going up to the trenches that morning ever returned again.

That afternoon the Prince had business at the Staff Headquarters out beyond Lowice, and I went out there in the automobile with him and Monsieur Goochkoff. We went through Lowice on the way there. The little town had been severely bombarded (it was taken two or three days later by the Germans), and we met many of the peasants hurrying away from it carrying their possessions with them. You may know the peasants of Lowice anywhere by their

More Doings of the Flying Column

distinctive dress, which is the most brilliantly coloured peasant dress imaginable. The women wear gorgeous petticoats of orange, red and blue, or green in vertical stripes and a cape of the same material over their shoulders, a bright-coloured shawl, generally orange, on their heads, and brilliant bootlaces—magenta is the colour most affected. The men, too, wear trousers of the same kind of vertical stripes, generally of orange and black. These splashes of bright colour are delicious in this sad, grey country.

The General of the Staff was quartered at Radzivilow Castle, and I explored the place while the Prince and Monsieur Goochkoff did their business. The old, dark hall, with armour hanging on the walls and worm-eaten furniture covered with priceless tapestry, would have made a splendid picture. A huge log fire burning on the open hearth lighted up the dark faces of the two Turkestan soldiers who were standing on guard at the door. In one corner a young lieutenant was taking interminable messages from the field telephone, and under the window another Turkestan soldier stood sharpening his dagger. The Prince asked him what he was doing, and his dark face lighted up. "Every night at eight," he said, still sharpening busily, "I go out and kill some Germans." The men of this Turkestan regiment are said to be extraordinarily brave men. They do not care at all about a rifle, but prefer to be at closer quarters with the enemy with their two-edged dagger, and the Germans like them as little as they like our own Gurkhas and Sikhs.

The next day the wounded began to arrive in Skiernevice, and in two days' time the temporary hospital was full.

The Tsar had a private theatre at Skiernevice with a little separate station of its own about 200 yards farther down the line than the ordinary station, and in many ways this made quite a suitable hospital except for the want of a proper water-supply.

The next thing we heard was that the Russian General had decided to fall back once more, and we must be prepared to move at any moment.

All that day we heard violent cannonading

More Doings of the Flying Column

going on and all the next night, though the hospital was already full, the little country carts came in one after another filled with wounded. They were to only stay one night, as in the morning ambulance trains were coming to take them all away, and we had orders to follow as soon as the last patient had gone. Another operating- and dressing-room was quickly improvised, but even with the two going hard all night it was difficult to keep pace with the number brought in.

The scenery had never been taken down after the last dramatic performance played in the theatre, and wounded men lay everywhere between the wings and drop scenes. The auditorium was packed so closely that you could hardly get between the men without treading on some one's hands and feet as they lay on the floor. The light had given out—in the two dressing-rooms there were oil-lamps, but in the rest of the place we had to make do with candle-ends stuck into bottles. The foyer had been made into a splendid kitchen, where hot tea and boiling soup could be got all night through. This department was worked by the local Red

Cross Society, and was a great credit to them.

About eight o'clock in the morning the first ambulance train came in, and was quickly filled with patients. We heard that the Germans were now very near, and hoped we should manage to get away all the wounded before they arrived.

The second train came up about eleven, and by that time a fierce rifle encounter was going on. From the hospital window we could see the Russian troops firing from the trenches near the railway. Soon there was a violent explosion that shook the place; this was the Russians blowing up the railway bridge on the western side of the station.

The second train went off, and there were very few patients left now, though some were still being brought in at intervals by the Red Cross carts. Our automobiles had started off to Warsaw with some wounded officers, but the rest of the column had orders to go to Zyradow by the last train to leave Skiernevice.

The sanitars now began to pack up the hospital; we did not mean to leave anything behind for the enemy if we could help it.

More Doings of the Flying Column

The few bedsteads were taken to pieces and tied up, the stretchers put together and the blankets tied up in bundles. When the last ambulance train came up about 2 P.M. the patients were first put in, and then every portable object that could be removed was packed into the train too. At the last moment, when the train was just about to start, one of the sanitars ran back and triumphantly brought out a pile of dirty soup plates to add to the collection. Nothing was left in the hospital but two dead men we had not time to bury.

The wounded were all going to Warsaw and the other Russian Sisters went on in the train with them. But our destination was Zyradow, only the next station but one down the line.

When we arrived at Zyradow about three o'clock we were looking forward to a bath and tea and bed, as we had been up all night and were very tired; but the train most unkindly dropped us about a quarter of a mile from the station, and we had to get out all our equipment and heavy cases of dressings, and put them at the side of the line, while Julian, the Prince's soldier servant, went off to try and find a man and a cart for the things. There was a steady downpour of rain, and we were soaked by the time he came back saying that there was nothing to be had at all. The station was all in crumbling ruins, so we could not leave the things there, and our precious dressings were beginning to get wet. Finally we got permission to put them in a closed cinema theatre near the station, but it was dark by that time, and we were wet and cold and began once more to centre our thoughts on baths and tea. We were a small party—only six of us—Princess, we two Sisters, Colonel S., a Russian dresser, and Julian. We caught a local Red Crosser. "Where is the hotel?" "There is no hotel here." "Where can we lodge for to-night?" "I don't know where you could lodge." "Where is the Red Cross Bureau?" asked Princess, in desperation. "About a quarter of an hour's walk. I will show you the way."

We got to the Red Cross Bureau to find that Monsieur Goochkoff had not yet arrived, though he was expected, and they could offer no solution of our difficulties, except

More Doings of the Flying Column

to advise us to go to the Factory Hospital and see if they could make any arrangement for us. The Matron there was *very* kind, and telephoned to every one she could think of, and finally got a message that we were expected, and were to sleep at the Reserve. So we trudged once more through the mud and rain. The "Reserve" was two small, empty rooms, where thirty Sisters were going to pass the night. They had no beds, and not even straw, but were just going to lie on the floor in their clothes. There was obviously no room for six more of us, and finally we went back once more to the Red Cross Bureau. Princess seized an empty room, and announced that we were going to sleep in it. We were told we couldn't, as it had been reserved for somebody else; but we didn't care, and got some patients' stretchers from the depot and lay down on them in our wet clothes just as we were. In the middle of the night the "somebody" for whom the room had been kept arrived, strode into the room, and turned up the electric light. The others were really asleep, and I pretended to be. He had a good look at us, and then strode out again grunting. We woke up every five minutes, it was so dreadfully cold, and though we were so tired, I was not sorry when it was time to get up.

We had breakfast at a dirty little restaurant in the town, and then got a message from the Red Cross that there would be nothing for us to do that day, but that we were probably going to be sent to Radzowill the following morning. So we decided to go off to the Factory Hospital and see if we could persuade the Matron to let us have a bath there.

Zyradow is one very large cotton and woollen factory, employing about 5000 hands. In Russia it is the good law that for every hundred workmen employed there shall be one hospital bed provided. In the small factories a few beds in the local hospital are generally subsidized, in larger ones they usually find it more convenient to have their own. So here there was a very nice little hospital with fifty beds, which had been stretched now to hold twice as many more, as a great many wounded had to be sent in here. The Matron is a Pole of Scottish extraction, and spoke fluent but

More Doings of the Flying Column

quite foreign English with a strong Scotch accent. There are a good many Scotch families here, who came over and settled in Poland about a hundred years ago, and who are all engaged in different departments in the factory. She was kindness itself, and gave us tea first and then prepared a hot bath for us all in turn. We got rid of most of our tormentors and were at peace once more.

As we left the hospital we met three footsore soldiers whose boots were absolutely worn right through. They were coming up to the hospital to see if the Matron had any dead men's boots that would fit them. It sounded rather gruesome—but she told us that that was quite a common errand. The Russian military boots are excellent, but, of course, all boots wear out very quickly under such trying circumstances of roads and weather. They are top boots, strong and waterproof, and very often made by the men themselves. The uniform, too, is very practical and so strong that the men have told me that carpets are made from the material. The colour is browner than our own khaki—and quite different both from the German, which is much greyer, and the Austrian, which is almost blue. I heard in Belgium that at the beginning of the war German soldiers were constantly mistaken for our men.

X

BY THE TRENCHES AT RADZIVILOW

THE next morning we went up to Radzivilow. It is the next station to Skiernevice, and there was very heavy fighting going on there when we went up. We were told we were going up on an armoured train, which sounded very thrilling, but when we got to the station we only found a quite ordinary carriage put on to the engine to take us up. The Russian battery was at that time at the south of the railway line, the German battery on the north of it—and we were in the centre of the sandwich. At Zyradow these cannon sounded distant, but as we neared Radzivilow the guns were crashing away as they did at Lodz, and we prepared for a hot time. The station had been entirely wrecked and was simply in ruins, but the station-master's house near by was still intact, and we had orders to rig up a temporary dressing-station there.

Field Hospital & Flying Column

Before we had time to unpack our dressings, a messenger arrived to tell us that the Germans had succeeded in enfilading a Russian trench close by, and that they were bringing fifty very badly wounded men to us almost at once. We had just time to start the sterilizer when the little carts began to arrive with some terribly wounded men. The machine guns had simply swept the trench from end to end. The worst of it was that some lived for hours when death would have been a more merciful release. Thank God we had plenty of morphia with us and could thus ease their terrible sufferings. One man had practically his whole face blown off, another had all his clothes and the flesh of his back all torn away. Another poor old fellow was brought in with nine wounds in the abdomen. He looked quite a patriarch with a long flowing beard —quite the oldest man I have seen in the Russian army. Poor Ivan, he had only just been called up to the front and this was his first battle. He was beautifully dressed, and so clean; his wife had prepared everything for him with such loving care, a warm knitted vest, and a white linen shirt most

By the Trenches at Radzivilow

beautifully embroidered with scarlet in a intricate key-pattern. Ivan was almost more unhappy at his wife's beautiful work having to be cut than at his own terrible wounds. He was quite conscious and not in much pain, and did so long to live even a week or two longer, so that he might see his wife once again. But it was not to be, and he died early the next morning—one of the dearest old men one could ever meet, and so pathetically grateful for the very little we could do for him.

The shells were crashing over our heads and bursting everywhere, but we were too busy to heed them, as more and more men were brought to the dressing-station. It was an awful problem what to do with them: the house was small and we were using the two biggest rooms downstairs as operating- and dressing-rooms. Straw was procured and laid on the floors of all the little rooms upstairs, and after each man's wounds were dressed he was carried with difficulty up the narrow winding staircase and laid on the floor.

The day wore on and as it got dark we began to do the work under great difficulties, for there were no shutters or blinds to the upstairs windows, and we dared not have any light—even a candle—there, as it would have brought down the German fire on us at once. So those poor men had to lie up there in the pitch dark, and one of us went round from time to time with a little electric torch. Downstairs we managed to darken the windows, but the dressings and operations had all to be done by candle-light.

The Germans were constantly sending up rockets of blue fire which illuminated the whole place, and we were afraid every moment they would find us out. Some of the shells had set houses near by on fire too, and the sky was lighted up with a dull red glow. The carts bringing the men showed no lights, and they were lifted out in the dark when they arrived and laid in rows in the lobby till we had time to see to them. By nine o'clock that evening we had more than 300 men, and were thankful to see an ambulance train coming up the line to take them away. The sanitars had a difficult job getting these poor men downstairs and carrying them to the train, which was quite dark too. But the men were

By the Trenches at Radzivilow

thankful themselves to get away, I think—
it was nerve-racking work for them, lying
wounded in that little house with the shells
bursting continually over it.

All night long the men were being brought
in from the trenches. About four in the
morning there was a little lull and some one
made tea. I wonder what people in England
would have thought if they had seen us at
that meal. We had it in the stuffy dressing-
room where we had been working without a
stop for sixteen hours with tightly closed
windows, and every smell that can be
imagined pervading it, the floor covered with
mud, blood and débris of dressings wherever
there were not stretchers on which were men
who had just been operated on. The meal of
milkless tea, black bread, and cheese, was
spread on a sterilized towel on the operating-
table, illuminated by two candles stuck in
bottles. Princess sat in the only chair, and
the rest of us eased our weary feet by sitting
on the edge of the dressing-boxes. Two dead
soldiers lay at our feet—it was not safe just
at that moment to take them out and bury
them. People would probably ask how we
could eat under those conditions. I don't

know how we could either, but we *did* and were thankful for it—for immediately after another rush began.

At eleven o'clock in the morning another ambulance train arrived and was quickly filled. By that time we had had more than 750 patients through our hands, and they were still being brought in large numbers. The fighting must have been terrific, for the men were absolutely worn out when they arrived, and fell asleep at once from exhaustion, in spite of their wounds. Some of them must have been a long time in the trenches, for many were in a terribly verminous condition. On one poor boy with a smashed leg the insects could have only been counted by the million. About ten minutes after his dressing was done, his white bandage was quite grey with the army of invaders that had collected on it from his other garments.

Early that afternoon we got a message that another Column was coming to relieve us, and that we were to return to Zyradow for a rest. We were very sorry to leave our little dressing-station, but rejoiced to hear that we were to go up again in two days' time to relieve this second Column, and that we

By the Trenches at Radzivilow

were to work alternately with them, forty-eight hours on, and then forty-eight hours off duty.

We had left Zyradow rather quiet, but when we came back we found the cannon going hard, both from the Radzivilow and the Goosof direction. It would have taken much more than cannon to keep *us* awake, however, and we lay down most gratefully on our stretchers in the empty room at the Red Cross Bureau and slept. A forty-eight hours' spell is rather long for the staff, though probably there would have been great difficulty in changing the Columns more often.

I woke up in the evening to hear the church bells ringing, and remembered that it was Christmas Eve and that they were ringing for the Midnight Mass, so I got up quickly. The large church was packed with people, every one of the little side chapels was full and people were even sitting on the altar steps. There must have been three or four thousand people there, most of them of course the people of the place, but also soldiers, Red Cross workers and many refugees mostly from Lowice. Poor people, it was a sad

Field Hospital & Flying Column

Christmas for them—having lost so much already and not knowing from day to day if they would lose all, as at that time it was a question whether or not the Russian authorities would decide for strategic reasons to fall back once more.

And then twelve o'clock struck and the Mass began.

Soon a young priest got up into the pulpit and gave them a little sermon. It was in Polish, but though I could not understand the words, I could tell from the people's faces what it was about. When he spoke of the horrors of war, the losses and the deaths and the suffering that had come to so many of them, one woman put her apron to her face and sobbed aloud in the tense silence. And in a moment the whole congregation began sobbing and moaning and swaying themselves to and fro. The young priest stopped and left them alone a moment or two, and then began to speak in a low persuasive voice. I do not know what he said, but he gradually soothed them and made them happy. And then the organ began pealing out triumphantly, and while the guns crashed and thundered outside,

By the Trenches at Radzivilow

the choir within sang of peace and goodwill to all men.

Christmas Day was a very mournful one for us, as we heard of the loss of our new and best automobile, which had just been given as a present to the Column. One of the boys was taking it to Warsaw from Skiernevice with some wounded officers, and it had broken down just outside the village. The mud was awful, and with the very greatest difficulty they managed to get it towed as far as Rawa, but had to finally abandon it to the Germans, though fortunately they got off safely themselves. It was a great blow to the Column, as it was impossible to replace it, these big ambulance cars costing something like 8000 roubles.

So our Christmas dinner eaten at our usual dirty little restaurant could not be called a success.

Food was very scarce at that time in Zyradow; there was hardly any meat or sugar, and no milk or eggs or white bread. One of us had brought a cake for Christmas from Warsaw weeks before, and it was partaken of on this melancholy occasion without enthusiasm. Even the punch made

Field Hospital & Flying Column

out of a teaspoonful of brandy from the bottom of Princess's flask mixed with about a pint of water and two lumps of sugar failed to move us to any hilarity. Our menu did not vary in any particular from that usually provided at the restaurant, though we did feel we might have had a clean cloth for once.

MENU

CHRISTMAS 1914

Gravy Soup.
Roast Horse.   Boiled Potatoes.
Currant Cake.
Tea.   Punch.

We were very glad to go up to Radzivilow once more. Our former dressing-station had been abandoned as too dangerous for staff and patients, and the dressing- and operating-room was now in a train about five versts down the line from Radzivilow station. Our train was a permanency on the line, and we lived and worked in it, while twice a day an ambulance train came up, our wounded were transferred to it and taken away, and we filled up once more. We found

By the Trenches at Radzivilow

things fairly quiet this time when we went up. The Germans had been making some very fierce attacks, trying to cross the river Rawka, and therefore their losses must have been very heavy, but the Russians were merely holding their ground, and so there were comparatively few wounded on our side. This time we were able to divide up into shifts for the work—a luxury we were very seldom able to indulge in.

We had previously made great friends with a Siberian captain, and we found to our delight that he was living in a little hut close to our train. He asked me one day if I would like to go up to the positions with him and take some Christmas presents round to the men. Of course I was more than delighted, and as he was going up that night and I was not on duty, the general very kindly gave permission for me to go up too. In the end Colonel S. and one of the Russian Sisters accompanied us as well. The captain got a rough cart and horse to take us part of the way, and he and another man rode on horseback beside us. We started off about ten o'clock, a very bright moonlight night— so bright that we had to take off our brassards and anything that could have shown up white against the dark background of the woods. We drove as far as the pine-woods in which the Russian positions were, and left the cart and horses in charge of a Cossack while we were away. The general had intended that we should see the reserve trenches, but we had seen plenty of them before, and our captain meant that we should see all the fun that was going, so he took us right up to the front positions. We went through the wood silently in single file, taking care that if possible not even a twig should crackle under our feet, till we came to the very front trenches at the edge of the wood. We crouched down and watched for some time. Everything was brilliantly illuminated by the moonlight, and we had to be very careful not to show ourselves. A very fierce German attack was going on, and the bullets were pattering like hail on the trees all round us. We could see nothing for some time but the smoke of the rifles.

The Germans were only about a hundred yards away from us at this time, and we could see the river Rawka glittering below in the moonlight. What an absurd little

By the Trenches at Radzivilow

river to have so much fighting about. That night it looked as if we could easily wade across it. The captain made a sign, and we crept with him along the edge of the wood, till we got to a Siberian officer's dug-out. At first we could not see anything, then we saw a hole between two bushes, and after slithering backwards down the hole, we got into a sort of cave that had been roofed in with poles and branches, and was absolutely invisible a few steps away. It was fearfully hot and frowzy—a little stove in the corner threw out a great heat, and the men all began to smoke, which made it worse.

We stayed a while talking, and then crawled along to visit one of the men's dug-outs, a German bullet just missing us as we passed, and burying itself in a tree. There were six men already in the dug-out, so we did not attempt to get in, but gave them tobacco and matches, for which they were very grateful. These men had an "ikon" or sacred picture hanging up inside their cave; the Russian soldiers on active service carry a regimental ikon, and many carry them in their pockets too. One man had his life saved by his ikon. He showed it to us; the bullet had gone just between the Mother and the Child, and was embedded in the wood.

It was all intensely interesting, and we left the positions with great reluctance, to return through the moonlit pine-woods till we reached our cart. We had indeed made a night of it, for it was five o'clock in the morning when we got back to the train once more, and both the doctor and I were on duty again at eight. But it was well worth losing a night's sleep to go up to the positions during a violent German attack. I wonder what the general would have said if he had known!

We finished our forty-eight hours' duty and returned once more to Zyradow. I was always loth to leave Radzivilow. The work there was splendid, and there more than anywhere else I have been to one feels the war as a High Adventure.

War would be the most glorious game in the world if it were not for the killing and wounding. In it one tastes the joy of comradeship to the full, the taking and giving, and helping and being helped in a way that would be impossible to conceive in the or-

By the Trenches at Radzivilow

dinary world. At Radzivilow, too, one could see the poetry of war, the zest of the frosty mornings, and the delight of the camp-fire at night, the warm, clean smell of the horses tethered everywhere, the keen hunger, the rough food sweetened by the sauce of danger, the riding out in high hope in the morning; even the returning wounded in the evening did not seem altogether such a bad thing out there. One has to die some time, and the Russian peasants esteem it a high honour to die for their "little Mother" as they call their country. The vision of the High Adventure is not often vouchsafed to one, but it is a good thing to have had it—it carries one through many a night at the shambles. Radzivilow is the only place it came to me. In Belgium one's heart was wrung by the poignancy of it all, its littleness and defencelessness; in Lodz one could see nothing for the squalor and "frightfulness"; in other places the ruined villages, the flight of the dazed, terrified peasants show one of the darkest sides of war.

* * * * *

It was New Year's Eve when we returned to Zyradow, and found ourselves billeted in a new house where there was not only a bed each, but a bathroom and a bath. Imagine what that meant to people who had not undressed at night for more than three weeks.

Midnight struck as we were having supper, and we drank the health of the New Year in many glasses of tea. What would the lifted veil of time disclose in this momentous year just opening for us?

It did not begin particularly auspiciously for me, for within the first few days of it I got a wound in the leg from a bit of shrapnel, was nearly killed by a bomb from a German Taube, and caught a very bad chill and had to go to bed with pleurisy—all of which happenings gave me leisure to write this little account of my adventures.

The bomb from the Taube was certainly the nearest escape I am ever likely to have in this world. I was walking over a piece of open ground, saw nothing, heard nothing, was dreaming in fact, when suddenly I heard a whirring overhead, and just above me was a German aeroplane. Before I had time to think, down came a bomb with a fearful explosion. I could not see anything for a minute, and then the smoke cleared away,

By the Trenches at Radzivilow

and I was standing at the edge of a large hole. The bomb had fallen into a bed of soft mud, and exploded upwards. Some soldiers who were not very far off rushed to see if I were killed, and were very surprised to find that I was practically unhurt. A bomb thrown that same afternoon that exploded on the pavement killed and wounded nine people.

The wound was from a stray bit of shrapnel and was only a trifle, fortunately, and soon healed. The pleurisy was a longer job and compelled me to go to bed for a fortnight. I was very miserable at being the only idle person I knew, till it occurred to me to spend my time in writing this little book, and a subsequent short holiday in Petrograd enabled me to finish it.

My enforced holiday is over now and I am on my way back to my beloved column once more—to the life on the open road—with its joys and sorrows, its comradeship, its pain and its inexplicable happiness—back once more to exchange the pen for the more ready weapon of the forceps.

And so I will leave this brief account of what I have seen in this great war. I know better than anyone can tell me what an imperfect sketch it is, but the history of the war will have to be studied from a great many different angles before a picture of it will be able to be presented in its true perspective, and it may be that this particular angle will be of some little interest to those who are interested in Red Cross work in different countries. Those who are workers themselves will forgive the roughness of the sketch, which was written during my illness in snatches and at odd times, on all sorts of stray pieces of paper and far from any books of reference; they will perhaps forget the imperfections in remembering that it has been written close to the turmoil of the battlefield, to the continual music of the cannon and the steady tramp of feet marching past my window.

Index

AEROPLANES, Taube, 145, 176
    throwing down proclamations, 53
Affiches, of the Burgomaster of Antwerp, 53
    of the Burgomaster of Brussels, 10, 11, 181, 182
    forbidding a menacing look, etc., 32
    German, proclaiming victories, 30, 67
    German, of Von der Golst, 67, 68
    instructions to citizens, 67
American Consul, help from, 66, 77
Antwerp, the forts of, 73
    the heavy guns, 73
    news of the downfall of, 96
Austrian prisoners, 148
Automobiles of the Flying Column, 146, 169

BELGIAN Red Cross Society, 5, 12
Bishop, sad fate of the, 103
Boden, a night at, 103, 104
Brassard, the Red Cross, 61
Brussels, fortifications of, 9
    German patients in fire-station hospital at, 20
    hospitals in, 13
    occupied by the Germans, 14
    the start to, 6, 7
Burgomaster of Antwerp, 53
    of Brussels, 10, 11, 54, 74
    of Charleroi, 20

CAMP, a German, 61, 62
Cannon, distinction between French and German, 40

Index

Cholera, rumours of, 97
Charleroi, burning of, 20, 22, 32
    and Charleville, 36
    terrorization of peasants in, 33
Christmas Eve in Zyradow, 167
    fare, 170
Cologne, arrival at, 85–87
Copenhagen, arrival at, 92

DANISH-GERMAN soldiers as guards, 81
Danish welcome, a, 92
Death of a Breton soldier, 44
    of a certain French count, 48, 49
Difference in French and German equipment, 47

ECHEVINS of Brussels, 74
Empress Marie Federovna, interview with, 111
Equipment of French and German soldiers, 47
Expulsion of nurses and doctors from Brussels, 80

FIRING at the Red Cross, 35
Fire-station hospital, 13, 19, 20
Flandres Libérale, 71
Flying Column, 125, 126
Fortress of St. Peter and St. Paul, 107
French convent, a, 60
    prisoners as patients, 28, 29

GERMAN officers' behaviour at Herbesthal, 83
    patients at fire-station, 20
    patients at M——, 41
    preparations for war, 33
    surgeon at M——, 31
Grand Duchess Cyril's Hospital in Warsaw, 144

HAMBURG, 88, 89
Hansen, Dr. Norman, 95
Harsh treatment of wounded, 42

Index

Haparanda, 104
Herbesthal, search at, 83
Holland, rumoured war with, 31
"Hoosh," 85
Hotel Cosmopolite, Copenhagen, 92
Hotel d'Europe, Warsaw, 124
Hotel at Lodz, 140

IKONS, 115, 173
Improvised hospital from theatre, 152
Infiladed trench, a, 162
Insects, 139
Inscription over gateway in Charleroi, 30
Interview with Dowager Empress of Russia, 111

ST. JOHN Ambulance Society, 5, 97
Jumet, the burning of, 21

KARUNGI, 104
Kiel Canal, 90

LIÈGE, 65, 83
Lodz, 131
    hospital at, 132-38
    shelling of, 132, 135
London, first week of the war, 2
Louvain, destruction of, 81
    refugees from, 11
Lowice, 150
Luggage problem, the, 126

MÂLINES, 60, 63, 81
M——— Red Cross Hospital, 23
    Committee, 28
    dinner-time, 27
    a night on duty, 23-24
  the curé of, 44
Max, Monsieur, 10, 11, 55, 74

Index

Maubeuge taken, 41
Münster, breakfast at, 88

NEUTRALITY of Belgium, 82
    of Denmark, 100
Newspaper boy caught by Germans, 71, 72
Night in the trenches, a, 171-74
Nurses in Brussels, 8, 19, 66

OPERATION, a severe, 25, 26
Ostend in August, 7

PATIENTS sent off to Germany, 41, 46
Petrograd, 107, 108
Pigeons, loss of, 55
Poem to British surgeons and nurses, 95
Poland, distress in, 97
Prisoners, Austrian, 148
    French, 28
    German, 148
Proclamation of Burgomaster of Brussels, 10, 11
    forbidding "a menacing look," 32
    German announcing victories, 30, 67
    of Von der Golst, 67, 68

QUEEN of Holland, 31

RADZIVILOW, 161
    Castle, 151
Raphael, St., 104
Rawka, the river, 172
Refugees from Termonde and Louvain, 11
    in Poland, 142
Registration of trained nurses, 4
Red Cross flag in Brussels, 55
    hospital in Warsaw, 113-21
    workers in Belgium, 23, 28, 46

Index

Russian factory laws, 158
Russian Red Cross, Committee, 108
 permission to serve, 97
Russian roads, 146
Russian sisterhoods, 109
Russian soldiers, 123
 their relationship with their officers, 123

SCARCITY of supplies, 24, 37, 169
Searched by German sentries, 62
Siberian ponies, 128
Skiernevice, 146
Skirmish between Belgian and German outposts, 59
Spies, 148
Stamps, issue of Belgian, 74
State registration of nurses, 4
St. Raphael, 104, 106
Stockholm, 102

TAUBE aeroplane, 147, 176
Termonde, refugees from, 11
Theatre at Skiernevice, 152
Times, the price of, 70
Tirlemont, 57, 82
Torchlight tattoo, 1
Turco soldiers, 29
Turkestan soldiers, 151, 152

UNTRAINED nurses, the danger, 5, 120

VENDRUP, 91
Voluntary Aid Detachments, 5

WALEHEIM, forts of, 73
Water-supply difficulties, 39
Warsaw, the city of, 121
 the Red Cross Hospital, 113-20

Index

Wavre St. Catherine, forts of, 73
Wounded French prisoners sent to Germany, 46
  German soldiers at M——, 41

ZEPPELINS, 81
Zouave patients, 45
Zyradow Hospital, 158

Printed by BALLANTYNE, HANSON & CO. LTD
At the Ballantyne Press
LONDON AND EDINBURGH